JEFFREY

SAAD'S

GLOBAL

KITCHEN

.
.
.

JEFFREY SAAD'S GLOBAL KITCHEN

:

RECIPES
Without
BORDERS

JEFFREY
SAAD

with
DEBRA OLLIVIER

PHOTOGRAPHY
BY AMY HEROLD

BALLANTINE BOOKS TRADE PAPERBACKS NEW YORK

A Ballantine Books Trade Paperback Original

Copyright © 2012 by Jeffrey Saad

All photographs copyright © 2011 by Amy Herold
for Amy Herold Photography

Published in the United States by Ballantine Books,
an imprint of The Random House Publishing Group,
a division of Random House, Inc., New York.

BALLANTINE and colophon are registered
trademarks of Random House, Inc.

ISBN 978-0-345-52836-0
eISBN 978-0-345-53218-3

Printed in China on acid-free paper

www.ballantinebooks.com

2 4 6 8 9 7 5 3 1

DEDICATED TO MY WIFE, NADIA,

WHO MAKES ME AND EVERYTHING I DO BETTER;

AND TO MY AMAZING CHILDREN AND ADVENTUROUS EATERS,

ISABELLA AND SEBASTIAN,

WHO WILL ALWAYS BE THE BEST THING

I HAVE EVER DONE IN MY LIFE.

TO THE COUNTLESS MENTORS, FRIENDS,

AND FAMILY WHO HAVE HELPED ME ACHIEVE MY DREAMS—

A DELICIOUS HEARTFELT THANK YOU.

CONTENTS

...

INTRODUCTION

...

Long before I was a "Next Food Network Star," I was a food nut and a heat-loving spice junkie. As a boy, I experimented with whatever I could find in our pantry and cook in our toaster oven. I fried, grilled, and melted anything I could get my hands on. (Epiphany #1: A cheese sandwich is infinitely better when it's grilled.)

Because I was raised—and generously fed—by my American mother and my Lebanese grandmother, my culinary adventures always involved a curiosity about tastes of the world. I developed a passion for vibrant international flavors. Heat and spice were a vehicle for this, and the endorphin rush I got from them corresponded to my desire for intensity in life and food. In many ways I was a typical boy who loved to run and play hard, but in the ballpark I was often more interested in the dog and the bun than the ball and the bat.

By the time I was thirteen, flipping burgers in a local diner, I knew food would be my life's vocation. Since then, I've fed friends, family, and communities; opened restaurants; and traveled around the globe in search of the spices and herbs that define the most flavorful cuisines.

In this book, I offer the recipes I've created along the way—delicious interpretations of regional dishes inspired by my journeys, my obsessions, and my enduring love of food and spices. Many people equate spices with spiciness, but spices are more about flavor—huge flavor. These supernovas of aroma and piquancy allow us to relish the world in a single bite.

Contrary to popular belief, you don't need fifty different spices and a master chef degree to use them. It takes only a few to evoke the world—simply. The trio of earthy cumin, citrusy coriander, and mustardy turmeric speaks Indian. Add cumin to brilliant red achiote, throw in some trusty Mexican oregano, a little lime zest, and bright cilantro, and your food will *habla español* to perfection. And if you combine caraway with cumin and coriander, the exotic flavor of North Africa will fill your palate.

As I explore on my television show, *United Tastes of America,* this nation will always have its regional distinctions (you'll always find killer gumbo in the South), but increasingly we all cook and eat in a global kitchen, and spices are an agent of change that brings those flavors to life. Each ingredient has its personality—from licorice-scented fennel to curiously sweet anise—and each has its partners. Knowing what spices to use is the key to importing world flavors into your own kitchen with inspired simplicity. My goal is to apply gourmet cooking principles to foods that speak an international language, bridge cultures, and reflect the world's palates. This is what you'll learn to do in these pages—to cook without borders—in ways that are easy to prepare and enjoy.

Jeffrey Saad

Every time you use a spice, you partake in a culinary and cultural history that goes back thousands of years. The quest for spices and other precious commodities kick-started the Age of Discovery back in the days of Columbus. Spice zealots explored uncharted seas and mapped the globe in the name of saffron, cinnamon, nutmeg, and pepper—that's how valuable those tiny gems of flavor were. Myths and wives' tales were also linked to nearly every one of them—put cumin in your lover's pocket and she would stay faithful forever; use dill to dispel bad weather and witches' spells. For thousands of years spices were used for their hugely potent medicinal and healing properties, and this continues today. Seasonings were added to many foods out of necessity. Techniques like pickling, salt-curing, drying, and smoking are no longer required to preserve food, but the unique flavors they impart are still some of our favorites.

WORLD PANTRY PRIMER

A well-stocked pantry is your base of operations. Whether your kitchen is the size of Nebraska or a tiny kitchenette with one burner, you can make fantastic flavorful meals with just a few essentials and key preparations.

1 | BE ORGANIZED. Before you start cooking, lay out all of your ingredients on your counter in the order you'll use them. If chopped shallots and garlic go into the pan first, put them first in line. If your recipe calls for olive oil and butter, put that on the counter. There's nothing worse than running to the fridge for an ingredient and having your onions burn when they're supposed to just caramelize. A bit of prep on the front end goes a long way in helping you save time, cook with ease, and enjoy the process.

2 | TRUST YOUR TONGUE AND YOUR NOSE. Cooking is a sensual process. Take a moment to be present with your food and really educate your palate. The tongue knows sweet, salty, sour, and bitter, and your nose can pick up aromas. Take a bite with your eyes closed and try to identify what you're tasting. In addition to recipe guidelines, these sensory tools will help you achieve balance, which is the foundation of great flavor.

3 | KNOW THY SALT. Used in the right amount, salt brings out the best flavor of each ingredient. But all salts are not the same. Kosher salt has a clean flavor and crystals big enough to see and feel between your fingers. Use it as often as you can. Snowflake the salt evenly over your meat, fish, and veggies and taste the natural flavors of your dish jump forward. Sea salt, with its deep mineral quality, is great for finishing off food before it's served.

4 | MANAGE THE HEAT WHEN SAUTÉING, ROASTING, BAKING, BROILING, AND BRAISING. Understand when to cook over low heat versus high heat. Using continuous high heat can burn food on the outside before its insides cook through. (Exception: Steak. See #5 below.)

SAUTÉING involves quick-and-easy high heat on the stove top, resulting in great color on chops, steaks, fillets, and thinner cuts of protein, as well as vegetables.

ROASTING is an ideal "surround-sound high heat" for slowly browning larger cuts of meat with high fat content, like a whole chicken, beef roast, rack of lamb, or pork loin. These meats need more time to cook in the center, but also beg for a deep golden brown exterior.

BAKING is "surround-sound gentle heat," best for lower-fat proteins like fish, or for pastries and scones, or for finishing off a chicken breast or pork tenderloin that was first sautéed on the outside for color but needs a lower heat and slower finish to retain its juices.

BROILING is the "sunbathing of cooking"—quick high heat on the top only. Broiling your dish (placed on the top rack of the oven) is the perfect way to toast bread crumbs after baking your mac and cheese, to make a golden cheese crust on the top of a lasagna, and to yield bread that is crispy on top but still soft in the center (see *Pan y Tomate* Tapas, page 102).

BRAISING is baking with liquid covering approximately one-third of your protein, to keep less fatty cuts of meat moist. Usually large cuts of protein with minimal fat need long, moist, slow cooking to soften their connective tissue (the elastic strands that make meat tough). Braising is great for shoulder cuts, leg of lamb, and Osso Bucco (page 70).

5 | PAY ATTENTION TO FAT. Generally, the lower a dish's fat content, the lower the heat you should use to cook it, because fat acts as a buffer to heat. A pork tenderloin dries out under high heat. A fatty cut of beef (or even a lean, succulent steak) cooked over high heat on both sides yields a thick, golden crust and a perfectly medium-rare center.

6 | GIVE YOUR MEAT A REST. After cooking, leaving your meat on top of the stove for fifteen minutes allows its juices to be reabsorbed. This way, the juices stay in the meat and in your mouth, instead of running out onto your plate.

7 | REDUCE FOR FLAVOR. A reduction is simply the result of boiling down wine or liquids—usually until you have half the amount you started with. When the water from these liquids evaporates, the solids—which hold the real flavor—are concentrated. Reducing naturally thickens sauces, intensifies flavors, and removes most of the alcohol.

8 | BE CAREFUL WHEN THICKENING SAUCES WITH FLOUR OR CORNSTARCH. But using too much starch can sometimes yield a bland taste and pasty texture. Before adding starches to your dish, mix them with a touch of water to create a slurry that you can easily whisk into your sauce. Start slowly and continually taste sauces thickened with these ingredients, and boil them until any starchy flavors disappear. If you add too much, you can always add stock, milk, or cream to thin out your sauce.

9 | COLOR EQUALS FLAVOR. Taste a slice of raw red bell pepper. Now heat some oil, drop in a slice of bell pepper, and cook until golden. As the color deepens, the pepper's strong, acrid essence converts to sugar, creating a natural sweetness. Likewise, the sharp taste of a raw onion becomes sweet and caramel—in flavor and color—when cooked.

10 | BALANCING FLAVORS AND TEXTURES IS KEY. Size *does* matter. Small is usually better. A small slice of red onion will add a palate-cleansing kick to a salad. The same red onion cut in a thick chunk will overpower the salad. On the other hand, a large chunk of boiled potato will have a richer, creamier center than a small one.

11 | GRIND YOUR SPICES FOR BOLDER FLAVORS. Think about the intense blast of flavor you get from the simple twist of a pepper mill. Now think about the flavor of pre-ground pepper. There is simply no comparing the flavor of freshly ground spices and their pre-ground counterparts. Whole spices contain precious oils that are released the minute you grind them, providing intense and aromatic flavors.

Pre-ground spices have their place in cooking, but they're far less potent and, in some cases, almost unrecognizable from their freshly ground origins, having oxidized long before their use. If you buy whole seeds and freshly grind them yourself with a mortar and pestle or in a small coffee grinder, they can be three times more flavorful than a store-bought ground spice and last up to four times as long, stored in an airtight container. Plus, it's so simple. Grinding your own spices is as quick and easy as grinding coffee beans.

12 | TOASTING SPICES intensifies their flavors, especially seeds like cumin, coriander, and mustard, which love to be toasted. The popular Indian spice fenugreek loses its bitterness and becomes mellow and rich. Ground turmeric comes to life. Black pepper becomes almost like a chile pepper spice when toasted. Sesame seeds become golden and sweet.

To toast, simply put your whole spices in a pan over medium heat and toast for about 2 minutes, or until you start to smell their fragrance, while stirring constantly to avoid burning. They will become slightly brown. Let the spices cool for about 3 minutes before grinding them. Toasting spices in a pan is also referred to as dry roasting. You can toast ground turmeric, garam masala, and smoked paprika in a little bit of canola oil or olive oil to wake up their glory.

13 | HERBS ARE BEST WHEN USED FRESH. Like spices, herbs are huge agents of flavor, full of precious oils, and are worlds apart from their dried, pre-ground counterparts. There's no comparing the deep green vibrancy of fresh basil, for example, with the relatively bland dried basil. The former has a deep green, sweet anise-scented vibrancy to it. The latter tastes like paper. Of course dried herbs have their place in cooking, especially in cuisines that historically called for them—like herbes de Provence, whose components are harvested when in season and then dried and used throughout the year. But choose fresh basil, cilantro, tarragon, parsley, mint, and, in some cases, rosemary, thyme, and sage, whenever possible.

All fresh herbs should be submerged in cold water, then pulled out and spun dry in a salad spinner or blotted well in a paper towel to get the dirt off prior to cooking or plating. This also keeps chopped herbs bright and full when garnishing a dish. One exception, however, is basil. Basil leaves can be used without rinsing since rinsing modifies their delicate nature and removes precious oils.

CHILES

14 | SPICE DOES NOT MEAN SPICINESS, but in the case of chiles, it does. For flavor, spiciness, *and* heat, we've got chiles. Chiles are the gatekeepers to your taste buds. The heat-packing power in chiles comes from a compound called capsaicin, and it varies along with the color and flavor of the chiles. Some chiles are mild and fruity. Others are crisp, grassy, and vegetal. Some are so hot they can almost melt your tongue. Others are happily mild. The best way to keep chiles fresh for the long haul is to put them in your freezer and simply grate them directly onto your food. It's as easy as that.

15 | SEEDS ARE THE SOURCE OF HEAT. The tiny seeds inside of chiles are responsible for the chiles' incredible heat and get bathed in capsaicin when you cut the chiles. By scraping out the seeds and the vein layer inside chiles, you reduce their heat. The more seeds you add to your food, the hotter it gets.

16 | DRIED CHILES ENJOY RICHER, DEEPER FLAVORS. Chiles are fantastically transformed when dried. Smoke and dry a fresh jalapeño, for example, and you get a chipotle. Do the same with a fresh poblano and you get an ancho.

Dried chiles can stay fresh at room temperature because most of their moisture is gone. I store mine in a jar in a cool, dark place and they last for months. You can also store them in the refrigerator if you have room.

17 | REHYDRATE DRIED CHILES AND WATCH THEIR FLESH AND FLAVORS SPRING BACK TO LIFE. To rehydrate, pull the stem off a dried chile. Shake out half the seeds or all of them—remember: seeds equal heat. Drop the chile into a saucepan filled with cold water and set it over high heat. Bring the water to a boil, turn off the heat, cover the pot, and let the chile sit for 1 to 2 hours until soft (not leathery).

Remove the chiles from the water and puree in a blender. This puree makes a perfect homemade chile paste.

And don't throw out the chile water—it's packed with flavor. Taste it. If it's not too bitter, use it as a stock to thin out your salsas or sauces for an even richer heat.

18 | CHILI POWDER AND CHILE FLAKES ARE WORLDS APART. Chili powder is generally made from anchos and other spices (paprika, dried oregano, cumin) and has a dark, smoky flavor. It's best cooked into a sauce or rubbed over meat before you barbecue. Chile flakes (also known as crushed red pepper flakes), on the other hand, are pure dried, crushed chiles (often chiles de árbol) that include heat-bearing seeds. They have a clean but powerful heat that almost adds an acidity and cleansing balance to dishes, without the smoky intensity of the powder. They also have the virtue of staying separate when you cook. Add a pinch of chile flakes to pasta with some shaved Parmesan cheese, for example, and you not only have flavor, but you have decorative red heat visually peppering your dish. Chile flakes are widely available in the spice section of most supermarkets.

19 | USE DIFFERENT OILS FOR DIFFERENT DISHES. Inexpensive regular olive oils are great for sautéing and grilling. Consider a more expensive, delicious, full-flavored extra virgin olive oil when making simple salad dressings (like lemon juice or red wine vinegar) or garnishing a bruschetta, or as a finishing drizzle on hummus or fresh vegetables. Generally, the more expensive the olive oil, the stronger the taste (spicy, green-olive peppery), so make sure you don't let the olive oil overpower your dressing.

Canola oil is great any time you need a cooking medium but don't need to add flavor, as is the case with Mexican cooking. It's also great for rubbing on the grill. (It has a higher flash point, so it can take higher heat than other oils.)

20 | THE MOST IMPORTANT TOOL IN YOUR KITCHEN IS YOUR HEART. Food is all about love and communion with people. It's the story of the world—of cultures, history, and geography—and the glue that keeps us together. Cooking with your heart and with passion is the true key to success and the best way to spread joy around.

JEFFREY

SAAD'S

GLOBAL

KITCHEN

SWEET
HEAT
MEXICO

. . .

PINEAPPLE-HABANERO SALSA 7

GRILLED CORN WITH CILANTRO PESTO AND COTIJA CHEESE 9

GRILLED ACHIOTE VEGGIE TOSTADAS WITH GOAT CHEESE 10

JEFFREY'S SPICY MARGARITA 12

ACHIOTE CHICKEN STEW WITH SPICY PICKLED RED ONIONS 13

TORTILLA SOUP WITH CUMIN-SPICED PORK 15

CRAB TOSTADAS WITH FIRE-ROASTED CHILES, AVOCADO,
AND TOMATILLO SALSA 18

ANISE SEED–CRUSTED TILAPIA TACOS WITH FIVE-MINUTE MOLE SAUCE 20

SEARED SCALLOP TACOS WITH GREEN CHILE CHUTNEY 23

ACHIOTE CHICKEN SANDWICH 25

No land has rocked my soul more sweetly than Mexico. I've traveled from Baja to Oaxaca and across the Yucatán Peninsula searching for the secrets to Mexico's sensational sweet heat, and found the most extraordinary food in the most ordinary places: small nondescript kitchens in rug-making villages, working-class eateries under freeway overpasses, and off-road beachside shacks. I've cooked with local chefs of all ranks, making masa, moles, and mezcal, whipping up gorgeous salsas from potent ripe chiles, and otherwise engaging in culinary acts of sweet, smoky, fire-roasted deliciousness. I was introduced to the amazing red annatto seed and became an instant devotee of this powerful little flavor igniter.

In Mexico wherever you go, delicacies come warmly wrapped in the superbly satisfying yet modest tortilla: from the *pibils* and lime soups of the Yucatán to the *barbacoa, pozole,* and *carnitas* of Central Mexico and the sensational seafood of Mexico's Caribbean-inspired southeastern regions. And like a tortilla, Mexican cuisine easily wraps itself around new tastes and crosses culinary borders.

Mexico's big flavors found their way so prominently into my cuisine that I named my restaurants in San Francisco Sweet Heat in homage to these radiant tastes. So it's only fitting we start our journey around the global kitchen here. *Buen provecho!*

ACHIOTE

CHILES

CILANTRO

CORIANDER SEED

CUMIN

MEXICAN OREGANO

TOMATILLOS

ACHIOTE is a fantastic Central American paste that hails from the brick-red **annatto seed.** It infuses anything it touches with sexy, bright red-orange color and subtle, smoky, peppery overtones and a slight nutmeg back note. Achiote instantly transforms five dollars' worth of bland chicken into a genius gourmet meal. Alone, it doesn't have much taste, but awakened with water or citrus, its flavor ignites. Use it as a paste or marinade for almost anything: seafood, poultry, vegetables, rice, stews—you name it. You can buy achiote in brick form (small and large) online as well as in most ethnic food stores.

CHILES dominate the Mexican flavor profile, coming in a staggering array of shapes, sizes, and intensities, ranging from mild to mind-blowing. Among my personal favorites: poblano, ancho (a dried, smoked poblano), jalapeño, chipotle (a dried, smoked jalapeño), guajillo, habanero, serrano, and Anaheim.

CILANTRO, grown from coriander seeds, looks like wispy parsley, but flavorwise it is worlds apart. Cilantro not only brings an unusual lemony, grassy bite that brightens Mexican and Asian cuisines and perfectly offsets heat; it also creates balance, like a slice of lemon in an iced tea. It's also visually beautiful, adding a decorative touch of flamboyant green to sauces, salsas, guacamoles, stews, stir-fries, and other veggie dishes.

CORIANDER SEED is a mini but mighty seed in the Mexican flavor family that also travels the world. Coriander adds a citrusy, aromatic element to food, and, like many spices, this bright sunshine seed is best toasted, then ground.

CUMIN is a culinary superstar. This potent aromatic seed has an earthy, peppery flavor that sweetly enhances almost any dish: veggies, meat and poultry, eggs, and sauces. (This versatility makes cumin a key element in other regional staples, like India's garam masala.) Fantastic ground or in seed form (see World Pantry Primer, page xi), this rich and fragrant supernova of flavor partners perfectly with coriander.

MEXICAN OREGANO is a softer, menthol version of the oregano we all have in our cabinets. It adds a warm and slightly bitter flavor to dishes like Achiote Chicken Stew with Spicy Pickled Red Onions (page 13).

TOMATILLOS lend a luscious tang to any meat, poultry, seafood, or vegetable dish. Cooking these small, lime-green fruits releases their piquant sweetness. In the gooseberry family, tomatillos are the base of uniquely Mexican salsas and sauces and appear in everything from guacamole to enchiladas, tacos, and Chilaquiles (page 201).

MEXICAN FLAVOR FAMILY

PINEAPPLE-HABANERO SALSA

Salsa is as classic to Mexico as chutneys are to India. Here, tangy pineapples meet spicy ha-banero chiles for the epitome of sweet heat. This hot, piercing salsa is the rage on everything and was in squeeze bottles on every table at my Sweet Heat restaurants. I created it for fish tacos, but it became a signature condiment. I couldn't make it fast enough!

SERVES 10

1½ cups chopped fresh pineapple
½ cup fresh cilantro
1 orange habanero chile, stemmed and chopped

½ cup chopped white onion
1 tablespoon fresh lime juice
½ teaspoon kosher salt
½ cup water

1 | Add the pineapple, cilantro, habanero, onion, lime juice, salt, and water to a blender and puree until smooth. (You can use canned pineapple, but a lot of the tangy freshness that defines this salsa might be lost.)

2 | Serve on fish, chicken, tacos, chips, or with anything else you like.

GRILLED CORN WITH CILANTRO PESTO AND COTIJA CHEESE

Unlike the classic Italian pesto, this piquant Mexican version with cilantro and pumpkin seeds creates a powerful flavor that's fantastic on corn as well as fish or chicken. Instead of serving the corn on the cob, you can cut the kernels off, sauté them, and then stir in the pesto for a great corn salad. Feel free to substitute Parmesan cheese if you don't have cotija, and use any leftover pumpkin seeds as snack food with a cocktail while the corn is grilling. The seeds stay fresh for a week if stored tightly covered.

SERVES 8

¼ cup green shelled pumpkin seeds

¾ cup plus 1 tablespoon canola oil

2 teaspoons chili powder

½ teaspoon kosher salt, plus more for seasoning

2 teaspoons finely chopped garlic

2 cups fresh cilantro, washed and large stems removed

½ cup grated cotija cheese, plus more for sprinkling (optional)

8 ears of fresh corn

1 | Preheat the oven to 450°F.

2 | In a small bowl, combine the pumpkin seeds, 1 tablespoon of the canola oil, the chili powder, and salt. Mix well. Spread the pumpkin seeds out evenly on a baking sheet and place on the middle rack of the oven. Stir the seeds every few minutes until they are golden brown and crackling, about 10 minutes. When the seeds are done, transfer to another flat pan to cool so they don't overcook on the hot pan.

3 | To prepare the pesto, in a food processor, combine the garlic, cilantro, the remaining ¾ cup canola oil, the roasted pumpkin seeds, and the cotija. Puree until evenly mixed but slightly chunky. Add salt, if desired. Set aside. (The pesto can be covered tightly in plastic wrap and refrigerated for up to 1 week.)

4 | To prepare the corn, preheat a grill to high.

5 | Husk the corn and place it on the grill. Leave the grill open and turn the corn every 2 minutes to evenly roast it all around, roughly 10 minutes. Char marks will let you know it's perfectly done. Use tongs to take the corn off the grill and place it on a platter.

6 | Using a pastry brush or butter knife, liberally slather the pesto over each ear of corn. Roll the corn around to completely cover it with pesto. Sprinkle with a little more cotija, if desired. Serve immediately.

GRILLED ACHIOTE VEGGIE TOSTADAS WITH GOAT CHEESE

I won my first episode of *The Next Food Network Star* with a variation of this dish. Mixed with citrus, the achiote infuses everything with a bright sunrise orange–red color and wonderfully pungent flavor, and pairs deliciously with the creamy, white goat cheese. It's sometimes tough to make veggies taste superb—feel free to substitute your own vegetables in place of zucchini or to wrap everything in a tortilla for the perfect burrito. This visual and flavorful feast won't let you down. For a touch of sweetness, you can add a teaspoon of agave syrup or honey to the beans. Enjoy with a spicy Margarita!

SERVES 4

¼	cup fresh orange juice	1	teaspoon dried Mexican oregano
¼	cup fresh lime juice	½	cup water
1½	tablespoons achiote paste	2	medium green zucchini, cut in half lengthwise
½	teaspoon kosher salt, plus more for seasoning		Freshly ground black pepper
2	tablespoons olive oil, plus more for rubbing	One	15-ounce can Bush's Best black beans, rinsed and drained
2	cups thinly sliced white onions	4	corn tostadas
6	ounces brown mushrooms, cleaned, stemmed, and cut in half	4	ounces creamy goat cheese
1	teaspoon cumin seed	½	cup roughly chopped fresh cilantro

1 | In a small bowl, mix together the orange juice, lime juice, achiote paste, and salt until smooth. Set aside.

2 | In a sauté pan over medium-high heat, add the olive oil. Add the onions and mushrooms and cook until golden, stirring occasionally, about 10 minutes. Add the cumin seed and oregano and cook for 30 seconds, releasing the aromas of the spices. Add the achiote mixture and water and stir well. Turn the heat to medium and cook for 10 minutes more, or until it reaches a sauce-like consistency. Remove from the heat and set aside.

3 | Preheat a grill to high. Make sure the grill is very hot so that you can get nice grill marks on the zucchini (otherwise it will be soft and overcooked).

continued

4 | Rub the zucchini halves with a touch of olive oil and season with salt and pepper. Place on the grill top (or in a broiler or sauté pan). Grill over high heat until marked on both sides but still firm. Cut the zucchini into ½-inch-thick pieces and set aside.

5 | In a small saucepan, heat the black beans.

6 | Lay the tostadas on a large platter. Top each one with the black beans and then with the grilled zucchini. Pour the onion mixture over each evenly. Using two forks, drop the goat cheese on top in small pieces. Garnish with the cilantro and serve.

Jeffrey's Spicy Margarita

Cut 1 orange habanero chile in half. (Avoid touching your eyes when you handle the chile.) Push the 2 halves into a bottle of Herradura Silver Tequila. Close the bottle and let it sit for at least 24 hours. (It can sit as long as you like—you don't ever have to remove the chile.)

In a shaker or pitcher, add a handful of ice, 1½ ounces spiced tequila, ½ ounce Cointreau (orange liqueur), the juice of 2 limes, and 1 teaspoon agave syrup or honey. Shake vigorously and strain through a fine-mesh sieve into martini glasses. Avoid aged tequila as the wood doesn't allow the full flavor of the habanero to come out.

ACHIOTE CHICKEN STEW WITH SPICY PICKLED RED ONIONS

This one-pot recipe yields a chicken that literally shreds apart in a luscious stew. Served on rice, it's a perfect meal for family dinners or parties. The next day relive the pleasure: Scoop it into tacos or a burrito, or eat it by itself with a green salad. This is one of those stews that tastes even better the next day (and the next) . . .

SERVES 6

PICKLED ONIONS

- 2 red onions, thinly sliced (about 4 cups)
- ½ cup fresh lime juice
- 1 orange habanero chile, seeded and finely chopped
- 1 teaspoon kosher salt

CHICKEN STEW

- Half 3.5-ounce box achiote paste
- ½ cup fresh lime juice
- ½ cup fresh orange juice
- 2 teaspoons kosher salt, plus more for seasoning
- 1 tablespoon canola oil

- 1 pound skinless, boneless chicken breasts
- 1 pound skinless, boneless chicken thighs
  Freshly ground black pepper
- 1 medium white onion, thinly sliced (about 2 cups)
- 1 teaspoon cumin seed
- 1 teaspoon dried Mexican oregano
- 1 quart chicken stock
- 6 cups cooked white rice
- 2 Hass avocados, each cut into about 12 slices
- 8 ounces cotija cheese, grated
- ½ bunch fresh cilantro, roughly chopped

1 | To prepare the pickled onions, place the red onions in a shallow nonreactive container large enough for the onions to be spread out thin. Add the lime juice, habanero, and salt and mix well. Allow to sit at room temperature for 2 hours, stirring every 30 minutes, or allow to sit in the refrigerator overnight. The onions are ready when they are bright pink and softened. They will be sweet and spicy with a little crunch.

2 | Preheat the oven to 300°F.

3 | To prepare the chicken stew, in a small bowl, combine the achiote paste, lime juice, orange juice, and salt. Using a fork, break the achiote apart and mix well until incorporated without any chunks. (You can also place the ingredients in a resealable plastic bag and mix them together.) Set aside.

continued

4 | In a large, wide pot over medium-high heat, add the canola oil. Pat the chicken breasts and thighs dry and season with salt and pepper. Once the oil is hot, add the chicken pieces and sauté until lightly golden on both sides; the chicken will still be raw in the center. You may have to brown the chicken in several batches based on the size of the pot. Remove the chicken from the pot and reserve in a baking dish just large enough to hold the chicken.

5 | In the same pot used for browning the chicken, add the white onion and cook until soft and golden. Add the cumin and oregano and stir. Allow to toast for 15 seconds, then add the chicken stock and the achiote mixture. Stir to mix well. Bring the mixture to a boil. Turn off the heat and carefully pour the mixture over the chicken in the baking dish. Cover tightly with aluminum foil and bake for 2 hours.

6 | Remove the baking dish from the oven. Shred the chicken in the broth using two forks. Once all the meat is shredded (it should resemble pulled pork), cover the dish and let it sit, allowing the chicken to absorb the sauce. The meat should be saucy, like a thick stew with just enough liquid to cover.

7 | Before serving, reheat the chicken in a pot on the stove. If it is not a nice thick, saucy consistency, simmer for a few minutes to reduce the sauce.

8 | Place the rice on plates as desired. Spoon the chicken with sauce over the top. Garnish with the sliced avocados, a forkful of the pickled red onions, and a sprinkle of cotija and cilantro.

FLAVOR SECRETS

This recipe is a quick, easy variation on cochinita *pibil,* a classic from Mexico's Yucatán region. Traditionally, a whole pig is rubbed in achiote, wrapped in banana leaves, and cooked in a hot rock oven until it falls apart. For an even more authentic version, substitute pork shoulder for the chicken. Cut the pork into large, wide pieces about 1 inch thick before following the chicken recipe, beginning with browning in a large pot.

TORTILLA SOUP WITH CUMIN-SPICED PORK

This tortilla soup has brought happiness to countless customers in my Sweet Heat restaurants. One of the delicious secrets here is the soft, raw corn tortilla pureed into the broth. It acts as a natural thickener while adding rich maize flavor and lots of texture. Think of it as the soup your Mexican grandma gives you when you're sick—but don't wait until then to make it!

SERVES 4

1	teaspoon cumin seed
8	ounces pork shoulder or tenderloin
3½	teaspoons kosher salt
	Freshly ground black pepper to taste
2	tablespoons canola oil
1½	cups thinly sliced white onions
2	garlic cloves, roughly chopped
1	teaspoon dried Mexican oregano
6	cups chicken stock
Two	6-inch corn tortillas

2	guajillo chiles or ½ ounce dried guajillo chiles
1	ancho chile or ¾ ounce dried ancho chiles
½	cup fresh lime juice
1	cup Bush's Best pinto beans, rinsed and drained
12	tortilla chips, crushed
3	tablespoons grated cotija cheese or grated Parmesan cheese
½	bunch fresh cilantro, roughly chopped
1	ripe avocado, cut into 16 slices

1 | Using a mortar and pestle or a coffee grinder, grind the cumin seed to a rough, sandy texture. Rub the cumin all over the pork, coating it evenly. Season with 1½ teaspoons salt and the pepper.

2 | In a pot large enough to brown the pork and onions at the same time, heat 2 tablespoons of the canola oil over medium-high heat. Place the pork on one side of the pot. Sauté, flipping frequently, until golden on both sides. Add the onions to the other side of the pot, but don't crowd the pork or it will braise instead of sauté. Once both the pork and the onions are browned, add the garlic and oregano and stir everything together. You want to bring the aroma out of the garlic, but you don't want to brown it. Add the chicken stock and ½ teaspoon salt to the pot and bring to a boil. Turn down the heat to a simmer.

continued

3 | Add the 2 whole corn tortillas to the stock, cover, and continue simmering. Be careful not to let the stock boil or the pork will get tough.

4 | Pull the stems off the guajillo and ancho chiles. Remove the seeds for a milder soup or leave them in for a spicy soup. Drop the chiles into the stock.

5 | Cook the mixture until the pork is thoroughly cooked, about 20 minutes if using tenderloin, or 90 minutes for a flavorful, tender shoulder.

6 | Remove the pork from the broth and set aside on a plate to cool.

7 | In a blender, puree the broth with all the ingredients that are in the pot. Pour the puree back into the pot so you can keep it warm, or reheat it if not serving it right away. Add the remaining 1½ teaspoons salt.

8 | Shred the pork using two forks. Add the shredded meat to the puree. Pour in the lime juice. Add the beans. (Since the beans are precooked, there is no need to cook them beforehand.)

9 | Ladle the soup into bowls and garnish with the crushed tortilla chips, cotija, cilantro, and sliced avocado.

FLAVOR SECRETS

Dried chile pods add a bigger punch of flavor and aroma than does chili powder. It is well worth the effort to use them.

CRAB TOSTADAS WITH FIRE-ROASTED CHILES, AVOCADO, AND TOMATILLO SALSA

I learned this recipe in Oaxaca on the dirt floor of a barn, using only one propane burner and a giant mortar and pestle. The tomatillos literally burst open to create a naturally thick, bright salsa. The smoky chipotle chiles—ancho and guajillo chiles work also—turn the salsa a rich green and add just enough heat to pull together the textures and flavors of creamy avocado, crunchy tostada, and tender crab. You can also substitute shrimp in place of the crabmeat for a dish that is great as an appetizer or a main course. And if you have any leftover crab mixture, combine it with the salsa and simmer it in a saucepan to make a filling for enchiladas.

SERVES 4 TO 8

1	red bell pepper
1	ripe avocado
¼	cup fresh lime juice
⅓	cup fresh cilantro, finely chopped, plus more for garnish (optional)
½	teaspoon kosher salt, plus more for seasoning

1	pound lump or backfin crabmeat
10	tomatillos
½	teaspoon cumin seed, toasted and ground
2	garlic cloves
2	chipotle chiles in adobo
6	corn tostadas

1 | Preheat the oven to broil.

2 | Place the red bell pepper on a sheet pan on the highest rack in the oven. Use tongs to turn the bell pepper every minute until it is completely black on all sides. (You can also blacken the bell pepper over an open flame on a grill—just be careful not to let it catch fire.) Place the bell pepper in a bowl, cover the bowl with aluminum foil, and let sit for 10 minutes to cool—this will also steam the skin loose. Once the bell pepper is cool, wipe off the skin gently with your fingers. Do not use water to get blackened skin off, the flavorful oils will get washed away. Remove the seeds and chop the bell pepper into 1-inch strips, placing the strips in a medium bowl. Set aside.

3 | Peel, pit, and chop the avocado into small cubes and add to the bell peppers. Add the lime juice and cilantro and season with salt. Stir well. Add the crabmeat and gently mix everything together.

Be careful not to overmix and break up the crabmeat. Cover the bowl and refrigerate until ready to serve.

4 | Remove the husks and stems of the tomatillos and discard. Rinse the tomatillos under warm water to remove the sticky film. Place in a medium pot and cover with cold water. Place over high heat and bring to a boil. Boil until the tomatillos turn dark green and are soft, about 10 minutes. Do not let them split or you will lose some yummy juice! Remove from the water and allow to cool. Discard the water.

5 | In a large mortar (you can also use a food processor), add the ½ teaspoon salt, the cumin, and the garlic and grind to a paste. Add the chipotles and continue to grind until smooth. (You can also use any dried chile: ancho, guajillo, etc. See page xvi on rehydrating dried chiles.) Add the cooled tomatillos. Press them gently between your fingers to pop them and then grind them into the mix. The salsa will be slightly chunky.

6 | Place each tostada on a plate or break them into 2-inch pieces to serve them appetizer style. Top the tostadas with the crab mixture. Drizzle the tomatillo salsa liberally over the crab. Garnish with additional chopped cilantro, if desired.

FLAVOR SECRETS

For an easy hot sauce, puree a can of chipotle chiles in adobo with a touch of water in a blender or food processor. Keep the puree in a tightly covered container in the refrigerator for up to a month. This is a great way to add a spoonful of quick, smoky heat to a sauce or salsa anytime. One chile equals about 1 teaspoon of the puree.

ANISE SEED—CRUSTED TILAPIA TACOS WITH FIVE-MINUTE MOLE SAUCE

This was the recipe for my first "Spice Smuggler" webisode on foodnetwork.com, and anise seed is the star. When paired with fish, anise seed yields a crunchy "breading" and a sweet licorice note. And this simplified version of mole sauce adds all the pleasure of a smoky chile flavor without all the work. The iceberg lettuce adds a fresh crunch to the tacos and balances the salty tang of the cotija cheese. If you don't have the dried chiles, substitute three chipotle chiles (canned) or 3 tablespoons chili powder for a megadelicious dish!

SERVES 4

1	pound tilapia	2	Roma tomatoes
2	teaspoons kosher salt, plus more for seasoning	⅓	cup skinless slivered almonds
2	tablespoons anise seed	1	teaspoon cumin seed
2	ancho chiles	¼	cup dark raisins
1	guajillo chile	8½	corn tortillas
2	tablespoons canola oil	2	cups shredded iceberg lettuce or red cabbage
1	cup thinly sliced white onions	¼	cup grated cotija cheese
2	garlic cloves		

1 | Season the tilapia with salt and lay it on a plate. Pour the anise seed over the fish (don't be shy) and turn the fish over to coat both sides evenly and liberally.

2 | Remove the stems from the ancho and guajillo chiles and add the chiles to a small saucepan filled with 5 inches of cold water. Bring to a boil, then turn off the heat and cover. Let sit for at least 15 minutes.

3 | In a large sauté pan over medium-high heat, add the canola oil. Once the oil is hot (you'll see a haze coming off the pan), carefully lay the anise-coated tilapia in the pan. Sauté the fish until golden on one side, about 2 minutes. Flip over and finish cooking, about 3 minutes. Remove from the pan and set aside.

4 | In the same pan, sauté the onions, garlic, and whole tomatoes until lightly golden brown. Monitor the heat so that you're always adding color but not burning anything. Add the almonds and cumin seed and cook for 1 more minute. Set aside.

5 | Place the soaked chiles in a blender. Pour 1 cup of the chile soaking water over the onion mixture in the sauté pan and discard the rest. Carefully transfer the mixture to the blender. Add the 2 teaspoons salt, the raisins, and the ½ corn tortilla and puree until very smooth.

6 | Briefly toast the remaining 8 tortillas on a grill or warm as desired and lay 2 on each of four plates. Spoon the tilapia onto the tortillas and break it up with a fork. Spoon the sauce over the fish. Add the shredded lettuce and garnish with the cotija cheese. Serve immediately.

FLAVOR SECRET

To gauge when fish is properly cooked on the stove top or grill, place a spatula halfway under the fish and push the handle down like a lever. If the fish separates, it's done. If it doesn't, continue cooking for a bit and repeat the process. When fish breaks nicely under a spatula inserted halfway, it's ready to serve.

SEARED SCALLOP TACOS WITH GREEN CHILE CHUTNEY

While tasting my way through Mexico, I had a seriously luscious scallop taco with chipotle salsa that made the rest of the world disappear for a moment. I loved the smoky heat of the sweet roasted chiles with the tender, lobsterlike texture of the scallops. Here, I sweeten things up by roasting green chiles with apple cider vinegar and sugar. The result is the first item featured on my Sweet Heat restaurant menu. Everything sits snugly in a warm tortilla topped with fresh crunchy shredded green cabbage. Heaven.

SERVES 3 TO 4

6	green Anaheim chiles	2	teaspoons dried Mexican oregano, toasted and ground
1	small jalapeño pepper	¼	cup apple cider vinegar
8	large sea scallops	¼	cup sugar
¾	teaspoon kosher salt, plus more for seasoning	1	teaspoon chipotle chile in adobo
	Freshly ground black pepper	½	cup sour cream
1	tablespoon canola oil	¼	cup fresh lime juice
½	teaspoon cumin seed, toasted and ground	6 or 8	corn or flour tortillas
		1	cup shredded green cabbage

1 | Preheat the oven to high broil.

2 | Place the Anaheim chiles on a sheet pan on the highest rack in the oven. Use tongs to turn the chiles every minute until they are completely black on all sides. (You can also blacken the chiles over an open flame on a grill—just be careful not to let them catch fire.) Place the chiles in a bowl, cover the bowl tightly with aluminum foil, and let sit for 10 minutes to cool—this will also steam the skin loose. Once the chiles are cool, wipe off the skin gently with your fingers. Do not use water to get blackened skin off chiles; the flavorful oils will get washed away. Remove the seeds and finely chop the chiles. Set aside.

3 | Finely chop the jalapeño, removing the seeds for a milder chutney or leaving them in for maximum heat. Add the jalapeño to the Anaheims and set aside.

4 | Rinse the scallops well and pat dry with a paper towel. Remove and discard the rubbery lip from the side of each scallop. Season the scallops with salt and pepper.

continued

5 | In a medium skillet over medium-high heat, add the canola oil. Once the oil is hot (you will see a haze coming off the oil), add the scallops to the pan. Sear on the first side until a nice golden crust forms, about 3 minutes. Flip over the scallops and continue cooking until the sides of the scallops turn from translucent to opaque, about 1 minute. Be careful not to overcook. Remove from the pan and set aside. The scallops will continue to cook when you remove them from the pan due to the residual heat.

6 | In a separate medium skillet over medium heat, add the cumin and oregano. Toast for 1 minute, just until you can smell the perfume of the spices. Add the vinegar, sugar, and ½ teaspoon of the salt and bring to a boil. Add the chopped Anaheim and jalapeño chiles and simmer until the mixture thickens but still easily flows from side to side as you tilt the pan. Using a rubber spatula, remove the chutney to a bowl and let cool. It will continue to thicken as it cools. (The chutney will last for 3 weeks in a tightly covered container in the refrigerator.)

7 | Smash the chipotle chile in a bowl. Use a fork to stir in the sour cream and the remaining ¼ teaspoon salt. Pour in the lime juice and mix well. Set aside at room temperature.

8 | Toast the tortillas on a grill, in a nonstick pan, or under the broiler until warm, soft, and slightly golden. Lay them on three or four plates. If not serving right away, place the tortillas in a bowl and cover with a dry towel.

9 | Divide the shredded cabbage evenly among the tortillas. Cut the scallops into pieces and lay them on the cabbage. Top with the chutney, then the seasoned sour cream. Enjoy!

FLAVOR SECRETS

For an easy and delicious salsa, take a can of chipotle chiles in adobo and puree with a touch of water in a blender or food processor. (Store in the refrigerator for up to 3 weeks.) Use a spoonful to kick up the flavor and heat of salsas, sauces, or salad dressings. Canned chipotle can be found in the ethnic food aisle of most supermarkets.

ACHIOTE CHICKEN SANDWICH

Achiote's bright, earthy flavor comes alive in this chicken sandwich kicked up a hundred notches. Fantastic for lunches, picnics, parties—anytime you want sensational flavor. And the leftover chicken and onions are great in tacos.

SERVES 6

1 tablespoon fresh orange juice	2 teaspoons canola oil
2 tablespoons fresh lime juice	Kosher salt and freshly ground black pepper
1 tablespoon achiote paste	
½ teaspoon cumin seed, ground	3 tablespoons mayonnaise
2 allspice berries or ⅛ teaspoon ground allspice	6 sandwich rolls, grilled or toasted, if desired
½ teaspoon dried Mexican oregano	3 cups shredded iceberg lettuce
½ pound skinless, boneless chicken breasts or thighs	2 cups pickled red onions (see page 13)

1 | To prepare the achiote marinade, in a medium bowl, add the orange juice, lime juice, achiote, cumin, allspice, and oregano. Mix well with a fork.

2 | Slice the chicken in half horizontally and place it in the bowl with the marinade, coating it thoroughly. Cover with plastic wrap and place on a counter for 30 minutes to 1 hour, or in the refrigerator for up to 6 hours.

3 | Brush a grill with the canola oil. Turn the grill to medium-high. (If you're cooking this on the stove top, heat 2 tablespoons canola oil in a medium sauté pan over medium heat.)

4 | Remove the chicken from the bowl. Wipe any excess marinade off the chicken and season both sides well with salt and pepper. Place the chicken on the grill and cook until the meat is white all the way through (160°F in the thickest part of the chicken, if using a meat thermometer). The breast will cook faster than the thighs. Keep in mind that the chicken will continue to cook a little bit as it rests, so be careful not to overcook it on the grill. Cut one piece open and peek if you need to.

5 | Remove the chicken from the heat and allow it to rest for 10 minutes.

6 | Spread the mayonnaise evenly over both sides of each roll. Lay the chicken on top of the mayonnaise on one half of the rolls. Lay the lettuce on top of the chicken. Spread the onions across the lettuce, close the sandwiches, and serve.

ROASTED, TOASTED, AND EXOTIC
MIDDLE EAST

. . .

The Middle East may be the cradle of civilization, but it's also home to spices that have traveled the world over.

As a third-generation Lebanese boy raised in Chicago, I shaked-and-baked American style at home, but my Lebanese grandmother—my beloved Sittee (that's "grandmother" in Arabic)—rocked my world with Middle Eastern cuisine. At Sittee's house, I'd graze on aromatic *sfeeha* (meat pies), fresh tabboulehs, roasted eggplant dishes glowing with turmeric, sumac-infused *fatayer* (spinach pies), and amazing Syrian bread salads. The scent of cardamom and rose water filled the air while her kitchen blazed. I couldn't even find Beirut on the map back then, but if you said *Lebanon,* I thought *food.*

Decades later something else lit me on fire, and it wasn't a habanero chile. It was Nadia, the love of my life, who was born in Iran and raised in Rome. When we married, I inherited a Persian mother-in-law, another *sittee,* who keeps the tastes of the Middle East constantly simmering in our home, sometimes in grand fashion. Persian New Year, or Norouz, for example, is a veritable feast of classics like *sabzi polo mahi* (green rice and fish) and golden saffron *tahdig* (see page 32). The culinary heritage of the Middle East, which is such a big part of my childhood, has literally fused its rich, savory stamp on my palate. I hope these recipes will do the same thing for you.

CARDAMOM

HARISSA

SAFFRON

SUMAC

TURMERIC

THYME

CARDAMOM is the "cologne" of spices. Its warm, musty flavor is also pleasantly medicinal. A spice chameleon, cardamom takes to sweet as well as to savory foods and is often found in Middle Eastern and Indian teas. Cardamom comes in pods, which can be ground or simmered whole in sauces (see page xiii and page 35).

HARISSA is the staple condiment of North Africa and a little tube of pure pleasure. This stunning, bright red paste is a blend of roasted caraway, toasted coriander and cumin, sun-dried tomatoes, and the fiery kick of chiles. An aromatic, moderately spicy paste, harissa warms the palate without overwhelming it. Spread it on steak, lamb, or chicken before grilling, use it to top vegetables, or add it to soups or stews. Harissa is also a scrumptious alternative to plain mayonnaise or ketchup. You can buy it in most supermarkets or online at www.kalustyans.com, for example.

SAFFRON is rich in historical lore and by far the most expensive spice by weight, because it is still farmed almost exclusively by hand. But you don't need much of it to infuse your food with its fragrant, dried-flower-like perfume and glowing yellow color. Saffron is incredible on fish and chicken, in sauces and vinaigrettes, in risotto or pasta, and, of course, in paella. Just about every world cuisine has a place for this precious spice.

SUMAC speaks Arabic like no other spice. It's a super-concentrated, purplish dried berry with a subtle floral flavor. Because of its slight astringency, sumac is sometimes used in place of lemon or vinegar. When blended with thyme and sesame seeds, sumac produces the exotic (and very Arabic) seasoning called zaatar. Sumac is used in spice rubs, marinades, and dressings, and is also served as a condiment throughout the Middle East.

TURMERIC has a complex, woody, slightly musky flavor with subtle hints of mustard and ginger. Like saffron, turmeric has a yellow color and a rich fragrance that marries well with various ethnic cuisines. It is an essential element in Indian curry powders, pastes, and masalas. Radiant to the max, turmeric makes even a humble egg dish glow with color and flavor.

THYME has more than fifty different varieties and is featured in foods around the globe. With a distinctly herbal aroma and a lemony taste, thyme complements dishes without overpowering other flavors. It is an essential herb in the bouquet garni that the French use to season stocks and soups, stews, and veggie dishes, and is a quintessential part of marinades worldwide, from French bourguignon to the yogurt dressings popular in Greece and Lebanon. Use it by stripping the leaves from their stems or use whole sprigs to flavor your soups and stews.

MIDDLE EASTERN FLAVOR FAMILY

HARISSA-ROASTED BABA GHANOUSH

Baba ghanoush is as classically Middle Eastern a dish as it gets. Adding my favorite North African chile paste, harissa, lends a blast of heat and a full-bodied kick that marry perfectly with creamy eggplant. Because cumin and caraway are in harissa, I love toasting and grinding a bit more of these seeds into the baba ghanoush—it's like hitting the turbo switch on a medley of fire-roasted flavors.

MAKES 2 CUPS BABA GHANOUSH

½	teaspoon cumin seed		2	tablespoons chopped fresh mint
½	teaspoon caraway seeds		1½	teaspoons kosher salt
4	Japanese eggplants		2	teaspoons tahini
2	tablespoons extra virgin olive oil		1	tablespoon harissa
1	tablespoon finely chopped garlic		6	whole pita breads, toasted

1 | In a dry pan over medium heat, toast the cumin and caraway just until you smell their perfume, about 2 minutes. Remove from the heat and let cool. Grind finely using a mortar and pestle or a coffee grinder. Set aside.

2 | Turn on a grill to high. Once the grill is hot, place the whole eggplants on the grill and rotate occasionally until evenly black. Set aside to cool. (If using an oven, place the eggplants on a baking sheet on the top rack of the oven. Cook at 500°F for about 15 minutes, rotating them occasionally, until black on all sides.)

3 | While the eggplants are roasting, in a medium skillet over medium heat, add the olive oil. Once it is hot, add the garlic and mint and cook for 30 seconds, just until you can smell the garlic. Remove from the heat and transfer to a food processor.

4 | Peel the eggplants and discard the skins and stems. Put the flesh (you should have about 2 cups) in the food processor with the garlic and mint. Add the salt, tahini, harissa, and ground cumin and caraway. Pulse-chop until all the ingredients are evenly mixed but slightly chunky, or puree them until smooth, if desired. Use a rubber spatula to carefully scrape the bottom and sides of the food processor bowl to ensure that the ingredients are mixed thoroughly.

5 | Put the baba ghanoush in a serving bowl and serve with the toasted pita breads. It can be stored in the refrigerator for up to 3 days.

ROASTED-GARLIC AND TOASTED-CUMIN HUMMUS WITH SMOKED-PAPRIKA PITA

This version of hummus features garlic which, when roasted, lends sweetness and creaminess as it disappears into the puree. The toasted cumin seed and smoked paprika breathe fire into the mild garbanzo beans.

MAKES 3 CUPS HUMMUS

1 large head garlic	1½ teaspoons kosher salt
3 teaspoons olive oil	¼ teaspoon cumin seed, toasted and ground
2½ cups Bush's Best garbanzo beans, rinsed and drained	¼ cup fresh lemon juice
4 teaspoons tahini	1 teaspoon smoked paprika
⅓ cup water	4 pita breads

1 | Preheat the oven to 400°F.

2 | Cut off about ¼ inch of the pointed head of the garlic. Lay the head on a piece of aluminum foil. Do not press the foil against the garlic or it will stick. Drizzle with 1 teaspoon of the olive oil. Bring the corners of the foil to the top to create a pouch. Roast in the oven until the garlic is dark brown and soft, about 45 minutes. Remove from the oven and set aside to cool.

3 | Squeeze the cloves of garlic into the bowl of a food processor and discard the skins. Add the garbanzo beans, tahini, water, salt, cumin, and lemon juice. Puree until smooth and creamy, at least 3 minutes. Run the food processor for at least another 3 to 5 minutes, to ensure the maximum creamy texture. Set aside.

4 | In a small bowl, mix together the remaining 2 teaspoons olive oil and the smoked paprika.

5 | Lightly toast the pita breads and set on a cutting board. Using a pastry brush, rub the pita with the smoked paprika olive oil. Cut the pita into triangles. Put the hummus in a bowl on a large platter. Lay the pitas around the bowl and serve.

FLAVOR SECRETS

For silky smooth hummus, blanch the garbanzo beans first. Drop them into boiling water for 1 minute, then transfer to an ice bath. Rub the skins off and discard.

CRISPY PERSIAN RICE (*TAHDIG*)

Two strong, colorful spices come together in this dish to create something even better than their individual attributes. Saffron delivers its brilliant shades of yellow, orange, and red color and its sweet perfume. Turmeric lends a mustardlike shine and a peppery, earthy quality. Basmati rice has a nutty taste and the perfect texture to withstand the heat in this process, and it caramelizes on the bottom of the pan as it cooks, creating a candylike lid for this Persian classic.

SERVES 6

¼ teaspoon saffron threads or powder
2 cups basmati rice
3 cups water

¼ cup plain yogurt
½ teaspoon ground turmeric
2 teaspoons kosher salt
6 tablespoons olive oil

1 | Soak the saffron in 2 tablespoons of hot water for 10 minutes.

2 | In a medium nonstick saucepan, add the rice. Fill the pot with cold water and then carefully pour out the water, leaving just the wet rice behind. Add the 3 cups water, the yogurt, saffron with its soaking water, turmeric, salt, and 1 tablespoon of the olive oil. Stir together and bring to a boil.

3 | Turn the heat to low and cover the pot. Cook until all the water is absorbed, 20 to 25 minutes. Uncover and, using the handle of a rubber spatula or large utensil, make five equally spaced holes in the rice, "drilling" to the bottom of the pan. Fill each hole with 1 tablespoon of the olive oil. Turn and tilt the pan back and forth until the oil completely disappears and spreads out across the bottom of the pan.

4 | Raise the heat to medium and place the lid on slightly ajar. Cook for 15 minutes. (Don't worry about not seeing the bottom of the rice as it browns—whether it's light or very dark golden, it will still be tasty.)

5 | Remove from the heat and let cool for 1 minute. Flip the pan over onto a serving plate and you will be rewarded with the golden, crispy rice now on top. Serve immediately with a stew of your choice (see Persian Beef/Eggplant Stew, page 36).

continued

You can let saffron sit for a few minutes in a few tablespoons of hot water before adding it (both the saffron and the water) to the pot for a more even distribution of the color and flavor. Grind the saffron threads in a cup of room-temperature water and keep it in the refrigerator for an instant saffron potion that will last indefinitely.

TABBOULEH BREAD SALAD WITH LEMON-SUMAC DRESSING

Tabbouleh meets *panzanella* and Lebanon meets Italy in this *Global Kitchen* original. Day-old rustic bread works the best, but fresh bread is fine for showcasing cardamom's spicy, herbal character and soaking up the vinaigrette. The lemon-sumac dressing brightens your palate with its dried berry flavor, and the parsley leaves are cut "chopped salad" style, giving you the full green, fresh flavor and texture unique to parsley. This is another side dish that can also be eaten as a vegetarian main course.

SERVES 4

⅛	cup bulgur	¼	cup plus 1 tablespoon fresh lemon juice
2	cups chopped tomatoes (½-inch cubes)	¼	cup plus 1 tablespoon extra virgin olive oil, plus more for drizzling, if desired
1	cup finely chopped green onions	1	teaspoon ground sumac
½	cup thinly shredded endive	½	teaspoon ground green cardamom
2	tablespoons fresh mint, thinly sliced	½	teaspoon kosher salt
2½	cups fresh flat-parsley leaves	½	teaspoon ground white pepper
		4	cups bread cubes (½ inch)

1 | Rinse the bulgur, place it in a medium bowl, cover with 2 inches of cold water, and let sit until soft but still with texture, about 1 hour. Drain and squeeze out the excess moisture.

2 | In a medium bowl (or food processor), mix together the soaked bulgur, tomatoes, green onions, endive, and mint. (If using a food processor, be aware that processing breaks down the herbs, creating excess moisture and muting the flavor of the greens.)

3 | Bunch the parsley leaves into a ball and cup your hand over them as if you are holding an orange. With a sharp knife, slice the parsley as thinly as you can. (Cutting parsley, green onions, and mint very thinly by hand will give you great texture that holds the dressing nicely.) Add to the bulgur-tomato mixture and mix well.

4 | To prepare the dressing, mix together the lemon juice, ¼ cup of the olive oil, the sumac, ¼ teaspoon of the cardamom, the salt, and the white pepper. Pour over the bulgur mixture and mix well to evenly coat. Cover and place in the refrigerator to marinate for 1 hour.

5 | Preheat the oven to 400°F.

continued

6 | Place the bread cubes in a large bowl. Mix together the remaining 1 tablespoon olive oil and the remaining ¼ teaspoon cardamom and drizzle over the bread cubes. Mix well to coat the bread cubes evenly. Spread out the bread on a sheet pan and toast in the oven until the bread is golden, about 10 minutes. Set aside to cool.

7 | Divide the bread cubes evenly among four plates. Spoon the tabbouleh mixture evenly over the bread cubes. Drizzle with additional olive oil, if desired. Serve immediately.

FLAVOR SECRETS

You can use pre-ground cardamom, but freshly ground cardamom is heavenly. Place the green cardamom pods in a mortar. Smash the pods with the pestle. As you smash them, the seeds will fall out and you can discard the husks. Grind the seeds to a powder.

PERSIAN BEEF/EGGPLANT STEW (*GHEIMEH BADEMJAN*)

This Persian delight features a tantalizing sauce created from a chicken stock base. The lentils are cooked in a rich tomato broth and the meat is actually a garnish—not a centerpiece.

SERVES 4

- 6 ounces yellow lentils (*chana dal*) or regular lentils
- 1 pound beef stew meat
- 2 teaspoons kosher salt, plus more for seasoning
  Freshly ground black pepper
- 1 pound Japanese eggplants
- 3 tablespoons olive oil
- 1 yellow onion, thinly sliced
- 1 teaspoon ground turmeric
- 1 cup tomato puree
- 4 cups chicken stock

1 | Soak the lentils overnight and then drain them, or cook the lentils according to the package instructions, drain, and set aside.

2 | Cut the beef into ½-inch cubes. Pat the beef dry with a paper towel and season with salt and pepper. Set aside.

3 | Cut the eggplants into 1-inch cubes and set aside.

4 | In a large low-sided pot over high heat, add 1 tablespoon of the olive oil. When hot add the beef. Sauté the beef until it is golden on both sides. Remove from the pot and set aside on a plate.

5 | To the same pot, add the remaining 2 tablespoons olive oil. Add the eggplants and cook until golden on all sides, stirring frequently. Remove from the pot and add them to the plate with the beef.

6 | Add the onions and turmeric to the pot and lower the heat to medium. Cook until the onions are soft and golden. Add the beef, eggplants, lentils, tomato puree, and chicken stock. Bring to a boil, then turn the heat to low, cover, and cook for about 1 hour. Add the 2 teaspoons salt, stir, and taste the stew and the meat. Make sure the meat is tender and the lentils are soft. If they're not, cook longer for desired doneness.

7 | Serve immediately, either alone or with traditional Crispy Persian Rice (page 32).

FLAVOR SECRETS

In the Middle East and other parts of the world, meat is often used as a condiment rather than as a main course. You get protein and rich flavor in a more healthy, savory, and economical way.

HARISSA AND GREEN ONION CHICKEN SALAD SANDWICHES

In North Africa, harissa is as popular as ketchup is here in the States, and for good reason. It instantly lends spice-laden, fire-roasted flavor to meat, as showcased in this recipe, where the chicken is poached (a healthy, if not mouthwatering, way to cook poultry). For more flavor, sauté or roast the chicken instead.

SERVES 4

2   tablespoons mayonnaise
1   tablespoon harissa
2   green onions, roughly chopped
3   tablespoons chopped roasted red bell pepper
1¼ teaspoons kosher salt
¼   teaspoon freshly ground black pepper

12 ounces skinless, boneless chicken breasts or thighs
1   tablespoon olive oil
2   tablespoons fresh mint, roughly chopped
1   teaspoon finely chopped garlic
4   sandwich rolls

1 | In a bowl, mix together the mayonnaise, harissa, green onions, bell pepper, ¼ teaspoon of the salt, and the black pepper and set aside.

2 | Fill a medium pot with enough water to cover the chicken by 2 inches. Add the remaining 1 teaspoon salt to the water. Bring to a boil, then turn down the heat to just below a simmer. Place the chicken in the water, making sure the water does not boil so that the chicken stays tender. Once the chicken reaches an internal temperature of 150°F or is firm and white in the center (not pink), remove from the pot and set on a plate to cool.

3 | Once the chicken is cool, shred it using two forks and add it to the bowl with the harissa mayonnaise.

4 | In a small sauté pan set over medium heat, add the olive oil. Add the mint and garlic and cook for about 30 seconds, just until you smell the garlic and the mint softens. You don't want the garlic to get dark or it will be too strong. Using a rubber spatula, transfer the garlic and mint mixture to the bowl with the chicken. Mix well to incorporate all the ingredients.

5 | Split open the sandwich rolls and scoop out some of the bread. Set aside for another use. Fill the rolls with the chicken salad mixture and enjoy!

HARISSA STEAK SANDWICHES

I made this killer sandwich on the finale of *The Next Food Network Star*. Fresh mint is a natural foil for harissa's heat, and the buttery sweetness of caramelized onions amps up its flavor. In this recipe (which can easily be halved) you can use watercress in place of arugula to kick this up a notch, or substitute spinach if you want less spice.

SERVES 4

One 10- to 12-ounce New York strip steak or steak of your choice (1 inch thick)

¾ teaspoon kosher salt, plus more for seasoning

½ teaspoon freshly ground black pepper

2 tablespoons harissa

Canola oil

1 tablespoon olive oil

¼ cup red onions, thinly sliced

¼ cup roughly chopped fresh mint

2 garlic cloves, finely chopped

¼ cup coarsely chopped sun-dried tomatoes

½ cup mayonnaise

4 sandwich rolls

1 medium yellow tomato, sliced into ¼-inch slices

2 cups arugula, washed and spun dry

1 | Season the steak with the salt and pepper. Rub ½ tablespoon harissa on each side of the steak.

2 | Rub a grill with canola oil and turn the grill to medium-high. Grill the steak for about 3 minutes. Flip it over and cook for another 3 minutes. This will yield a medium-rare steak, depending on the thickness of the meat. Adjust the timing for the desired doneness and the thickness of the steak. Set aside for at least 10 minutes to allow the juices to reabsorb.

3 | In a small sauté pan over medium heat, add the olive oil. Once the oil is hot, add the onions, mint, and garlic. Cook for 30 seconds, just until you can smell the perfume of the garlic and the onions and mint start to soften. (If the mint and garlic brown, they yield a less subtle, toasted flavor.) Add the sun-dried tomatoes and a pinch of salt. Turn off the heat and stir. Remove the mixture to a medium bowl. Extract the onions to a plate.

4 | Stir the mayonnaise into the sun-dried tomato mixture. Stir in the remaining 1 tablespoon harissa and mix well.

5 | Grill or toast the rolls, if you like. Spread the flavored mayonnaise on both sides of the rolls. Slice the steak at a 45-degree angle into ⅓-inch-thick slices and lay them across the rolls. Top with reserved onions, the sliced yellow tomatoes, and the arugula. Serve immediately.

SUMAC-GRILLED SALMON WITH THYME, TOASTED SESAME SEEDS, AND LEMON

The bright citrus of lemon heightens the herbal flavors of sumac and the peanut-buttery richness of the sesame seeds in this savory Middle Eastern dish. Great with vegetables, over rice, or in a pita bread.

SERVES 4

1	teaspoon ground sumac	1	tablespoon sesame seeds
1½	teaspoons dried thyme	1	cup sliced tomatoes (⅓-inch slices)
1½	teaspoons kosher salt	1	cup thinly sliced yellow onions
1	tablespoon plus 2 teaspoons olive oil		Canola oil
One	1½-pound salmon fillet, skin removed	1	lemon, quartered

1 | In a small bowl, mix together the sumac, 1 teaspoon of the thyme, 1 teaspoon of the salt, and 2 teaspoons of the olive oil. Rub all over the salmon and let sit at room temperature for 30 minutes to 1 hour.

2 | In a small pan over medium heat, toss and cook the sesame seeds until golden. Pour into a bowl and set aside.

3 | In a medium skillet over medium heat, add the remaining 1 tablespoon olive oil. Once the oil is hot, add the tomatoes, onions, the remaining ½ teaspoon thyme, and the remaining ½ teaspoon salt. Toss and cook until golden, about 5 minutes. Set aside.

4 | Rub a grill with canola oil and turn the grill to medium-high. (If cooking indoors, move a rack to the top of the oven—about 4 inches from the heat—and turn the broiler to low.) Place the salmon on the grill, flesh side down. (Do not touch until it has cooked. This will allow it to sear and not stick.) Once well marked on the grill, rotate the salmon a one-third turn on the same side. This will give you X marks on the salmon. Flip the salmon over and cook until it is medium-rare, about 3 minutes, or to desired doneness. Slide a spatula under the fish to the center. Push the handle down to separate the fish on top. You'll be able to see if the center is pink or medium-rare.

5 | Spread the tomato-onion mixture on a platter. Set the salmon on top and garnish with the toasted sesame seeds and lemon. Enjoy.

BEEF KEBABS WITH SUMAC AND ROASTED TOMATO RICE

I learned about sumac from my mother-in-law, who introduced me to it in a shaker on the table of a Persian restaurant. Although this berry-saturated spice is a natural flavoring for meat, vegetables are an incredible substitute. Simply swap out the cubed steak for cauliflower or zucchini for an equally savory delight. These kebabs go great with Sumac and Toasted Oregano Cucumber Yogurt Dip.

SERVES 4

2 cups basmati rice	1 teaspoon dried thyme
3 cups water	2 tablespoons sesame oil
2½ teaspoons kosher salt, plus more for seasoning	One 1½-pound rib-eye steak or beef of your choice, cut into 1½-inch cubes
4 tablespoons olive oil	Canola oil
½ teaspoon ground turmeric	¼ teaspoon freshly ground black pepper, plus more for seasoning
1 large red onion	
1 large red bell pepper	2 cups cherry tomatoes
1 large pasilla chile or green bell pepper	½ teaspoon ground sumac
16 brown mushrooms	2 tablespoons fresh flat-leaf parsley, roughly chopped

1 | Rinse the rice with cold water, then place it in a medium pot. Add the water, 2 teaspoons of the salt, 2 tablespoons of the olive oil, and the turmeric. Place the pot over high heat and bring to a boil. Cover and turn down the heat to low. Cook until tender, about 20 minutes. Remove from the heat and set aside until ready to eat.

2 | While the rice is cooking (or the night before using), prepare the marinade. Peel the red onion and pull apart the layers. Cut into roughly 1-inch-thick slices and place in a large bowl. Cut the red bell pepper and pasilla chile in half and then roughly chop into 1-inch-thick slices. Add to the bowl with the red onions. Rinse the mushrooms and pat dry. Cut off and discard the thickest part of the stems. Add the mushrooms to the onions, bell peppers, and chile. Add the thyme, sesame oil, and 1 tablespoon of the remaining olive oil and mix well.

3 | Pat the meat dry with a paper towel, then place in the bowl with the marinade. Use your hands to thoroughly coat the meat evenly.

4 | Using 4 large metal skewers, or 12 smaller wooden skewers soaked in water for 30 minutes (to prevent burning), alternately slide the meat and marinated vegetables onto each skewer. Be sure to leave a small space between the items so that everything cooks evenly.

5 | Rub the grill with canola oil and turn the grill to medium-high. (If cooking indoors, move a rack to the top of the oven—about 4 inches from the heat—and turn the broiler to low.) Let heat while seasoning the skewers.

6 | Season the skewers with salt and black pepper (don't be shy). Place the skewers on the grill or under the broiler and cook, rotating the skewers every few minutes until the meat is cooked to the desired doneness, about 8 minutes total for medium-rare.

7 | Heat the oven to 400°F. (Be sure the kebabs are cooked thoroughly and removed if using the same oven to broil the skewers, too.)

8 | Toss together the cherry tomatoes, the remaining 1 tablespoon olive oil, the sumac, the remaining ½ teaspoon salt, and the black pepper in a baking dish. Place in the oven and roast until the tomatoes are golden but before they burst, about 15 minutes. Set aside.

9 | Divide the rice among serving plates. Scatter the roasted tomatoes across the rice. Place the kebabs on top. Garnish with the chopped parsley and serve.

Sumac and Toasted Oregano Cucumber Yogurt Dip

Peel 2 cucumbers and cut each into 4 long strips. Cut each strip into ½-inch cubes and place in a large bowl. Add 2 teaspoons ground sumac and 2 teaspoons kosher salt and stir to mix well. Allow the cucumbers to sit at room temperature for 15 minutes.

In a dry skillet over medium heat, add 4 teaspoons sesame seeds and 2 teaspoons dried thyme. Toast until the sesame seeds are golden and you can smell the thyme, about 1 minute. Remove from the heat and add to the cucumbers. Add 1 tablespoon olive oil and 2 teaspoons roughly chopped fresh mint, and stir. Let sit for another 5 minutes. Stir in 2 cups plain whole-milk yogurt and serve immediately. *(Makes 3 cups)*

SUMAC-SPICED KIBBEE

My sittee used to make kibbee all the time when I was kid. Though she made hers in a large baking dish about two inches deep and cut the kibbee into diamond shapes, here I use muffin cups because it's super practical. The bulgur soaks up the savory liquid, adding texture and flavor without dominating the dish. (Thank you for the inspiration, Sittee!)

SERVES 4

½ cup bulgur	¾ pound ground lamb
⅓ cup plus ½ cup pine nuts	¾ pound ground beef (15% fat)
2 medium leeks	⅓ cup finely chopped shallots
4 tablespoons olive oil	¼ teaspoon ground allspice
1 teaspoon unsalted butter	2 teaspoons dried thyme
1 teaspoon cumin seed, ground	1 tablespoon finely chopped garlic
2½ teaspoons sumac, ground	2 tablespoons finely chopped fresh mint
1½ teaspoons white pepper, ground	1 cup plain yogurt
3¼ teaspoons kosher salt	

1 | Rinse the bulgur, place in a pot and cover with 2 inches of cold water, and let sit until soft but still with texture, about 1 hour. Drain and squeeze out any excess moisture.

2 | In a dry pan set over medium heat, toast ⅓ cup of the pine nuts until golden, about 2 minutes. Remove from the heat, transfer to a small bowl, and set aside. Roughly chop the remaining ½ cup pine nuts and set aside.

3 | Cut the leeks in half and rinse under cold water. Lift out and remove the hard core. Discard the core, along with the dark green parts of the leeks. Chop the remaining white leek very finely. You should have 1 cup of finely chopped leeks.

4 | In a small skillet over medium heat, add 1 tablespoon of the olive oil and the butter. Once they are hot, add ½ cup of the chopped leeks, ½ teaspoon of the cumin, 1½ teaspoons of the sumac, ½ teaspoon of the white pepper, and 1½ teaspoons of the salt. Cook until the leeks are soft and barely golden. You don't want crispy leeks. Remove from the heat and set aside to cool.

5 | In a bowl, mix together ¼ pound of the ground lamb, ¼ pound of the ground beef, and the cooled cooked leeks. Set aside. This is your pressed meat filling.

6 | In a medium skillet over medium heat, add 1 tablespoon of the remaining olive oil. Once the oil is hot, add the remaining ½ cup chopped leeks, ½ teaspoon cumin, 1 teaspoon sumac, 1 teaspoon white pepper, 1½ teaspoons of the remaining salt, the shallots, and the allspice. Cook until the leeks and shallots are soft but not colored. Remove from the heat and set aside to cool.

7 | In a bowl, mix together the remaining ½ pound ground lamb, remaining ½ pound ground beef, bulgur, and leek-shallot mixture. This is your bulgur-meat base.

8 | Heat the oven to 400°F. Have ready a 12-cup nonstick muffin tin. You will use 10 cups; 2 cups will be empty.

9 | Divide the pressed meat base in half. Use half to create a bottom layer in each of 10 muffin cups, pressing down gently. Sprinkle the toasted pine nuts in a single layer in each muffin cup. Then put in the bulgur-meat filling and distribute it evenly, without pressing down, creating a crumbly beef center. Use your hands to press together the remaining half of the pressed meat base. Break off a piece and place it on the top of each of the 10 muffin cups.

10 | Using a butter knife, make a ¼-inch-deep X incision on the top of each cup. This will allow the garnish and oil to collect and get golden while the kibbee bake. Sprinkle the tops with the chopped pine nuts and the thyme. Drizzle with 1 more tablespoon of the remaining olive oil.

11 | Place the muffin tin on the center rack of the oven and bake for about 12 minutes, or until the center reads 125°F on a meat thermometer. Remove from the oven and let sit for 15 minutes.

12 | Meanwhile, in a small skillet set over medium heat, add the remaining 1 tablespoon olive oil. Once the oil is hot, add the garlic and mint and cook for 30 seconds. Remove from the heat and transfer to a bowl. Mix in the yogurt and the remaining ¼ teaspoon salt. Spoon the sauce on top of the individual kibbees or serve on the side for dipping with anything you like. Serve immediately.

FLAVOR SECRETS

Freshly ground meat is always far more flavorful than prepackaged meat. Ask the butcher at your local supermarket or butcher shop to grind it for you.

BUON APPETITO ITALY

...

CLASSIC TOMATO-BASIL BRUSCHETTA 52

BUTTERNUT SQUASH AND ROASTED BRUSSELS SPROUTS RISOTTO 53

WHITE BEAN SOUP WITH ROSEMARY PESTO 56

GORGONZOLA, CARAMELIZED PEAR, AND GOAT CHEESE SANDWICH 57

FARFALLE WITH BLACK OLIVES, SHAVED PECORINO, AND LEMON 60

OPEN-FACE LASAGNA WITH MOREL MUSHROOMS AND ASPARAGUS 62

**FUSILLI WITH FENNEL SEED—OREGANO CHICKEN,
MUSHROOMS, AND CREAM SAUCE 64**

PORK CHOPS WITH CARAMELIZED APPLES AND ARUGULA 66

PENNE BOLOGNESE 68

OSSO BUCCO 70

The flavors of Italy are bright and full of life, just like Italians. And they're as much about the woody aromatics of herbs as they are about seeds and spices. Herbs create a fresh green flavor contrast to the rich, tomato-and-cheesy heft of Italian cuisine.

My wife and culinary cohort, Nadia, was raised in Rome, and she's brought to life for me both the simple and the seductive nature of Italian cuisine. On a trip to her hometown she introduced me to the sandwich she grew up on—sweet-and-salty, cave-aged prosciutto and creamy mozzarella between pillow-soft layers of white bread—and together we wolfed down slices of square pizza off sheet pans in tiny hole-in-the-wall shops. There was nothing we didn't eat in this land that brought us fusilli and farfalle, lasagna and linguine, bowties and bucatini, macaroni and manicotti, ravioli and rigatoni—to name just a few.

Italy is a culinary mecca so enticing that, after opening my Sweet Heat restaurants in San Francisco, I turned my culinary compass around and joined the team of Pasta Pomodoro. Working with the incomparable Adriano Paganini, I helped bring more of Italy's most delicious comfort food to America.

These dishes are but a small sampling of big, Italian-inspired delights—with international twists. *Buon appetito!*

BASIL
CHILE FLAKES
FENNEL SEED
OREGANO
ROSEMARY
SAGE

BASIL—and herbs in general—is the corner-stone of Italian cuisine. There is no Caprese salad or pesto without it. It is the tomato's best friend and brings its refreshing, almost aniselike warmth to countless dishes. Basil should always be used fresh. Comparatively speaking, dried basil is like eating paper.

CHILE FLAKES (widely known as crushed red pepper flakes) are gorgeous miniature flecks of pure heat, usually made from dried chiles de árbol. Adding chile flakes to the nutty, mouthwatering tang of, say, Parmesan cheese is all you need to get awesome flavor contrast and lovely, decorative bursts of red.

FENNEL SEEDS have the same licorice snap of its sister, the anise seed, but it is notably more subtle. Fennel seed is responsible for the mouth-puckering taste in Italian salamis and is one of the main components of the once-popular liquor called absinthe. Add fennel seed to meat and vegetable dishes for an unmistakably European flavor.

OREGANO is an exceptional herb with a slightly bitter flavor. It can be more potent when dried than when fresh. Oregano finds its way all around the Mediterranean, from Italy to Greece and beyond.

ROSEMARY can be used fresh or dried, but its deep floral flavor is most potent when used fresh. But be careful: This pungent herb can ruin a dish and make it taste like bitter medicine if you use too much of it. Like thyme, you can strip the leaves from the stems, or like a bay leaf, use the whole sprig to flavor your food (just remember to remove them before serving). Rosemary is great with almost everything: lamb, chicken, and pork dishes, as well as vegetables, pastas, and breads.

SAGE has a stronger flavor profile than other herbs, so it's best used sparingly. It can be used fresh or dried and adds another slightly bitter, woody layer of taste to cheese, vegetable dishes, and grilled meats. It's also an essential element in flavoring foods like butternut squash and stuffings of all sorts.

ITALIAN FLAVOR FAMILY

CLASSIC TOMATO-BASIL BRUSCHETTA

This beautiful classic represents everything simple and wonderful about Italian cooking. Everyone loves bruschetta. It's easy to make and highlights the freshness and pure flavors of its toppings. Try to get lusciously sweet ripe tomatoes, bright basil, fresh garlic, and the best olive oil you can afford.

SERVES 8

4 cups cubed tomatoes (½-inch cubes)	1 teaspoon kosher salt
½ cup fresh basil	¼ cup extra virgin olive oil
2 teaspoons finely minced garlic	1 loaf rustic Italian bread, cut into 8 slices

1 | Place the tomatoes in a wide bowl to allow even marinating. On a cutting board, lay the basil leaves on top of one another in a stack. Fold the stack in half and cut the basil into thin ribbons. Cut the piles of ribbons in half. This will give you nice strands of green basil. (Overchopping basil will turn it black.) Add the basil to the bowl along with the garlic, salt, and olive oil, and mix together. (Make sure the garlic is very finely minced so it blends in and flavors the tomatoes. If the mince is too large, the garlic is "hot" and overwhelming.) Let the mixture sit for 20 minutes at room temperature.

2 | Grill the bread in a grill press or toast it under the broiler. Place the bread on a platter and top with heaping tablespoonfuls of the tomato mixture. (Rustic bread has large pores and a thick, chewy crust that holds up well to the tomato mixture.)

BUTTERNUT SQUASH AND ROASTED BRUSSELS SPROUTS RISOTTO

Making risotto requires care but is worth every minute of attention. Essentially, it involves a series of reductions—precisely measured portions of stock boiled down to concentrate the flavor into the rice, creating a thick, creamy consistency. Use a low-sodium or homemade chicken stock so it doesn't get too salty as it reduces. This savory pillow of al dente risotto enriches the flavor of the sweet butternut squash. (It's important to cut the squash into small enough pieces that it gets tender and golden. If the cubes are too big, they will still be hard inside, even when golden on the outside.)

SERVES 4

2	cups water
6	cups low-sodium or homemade chicken stock
3½	tablespoons olive oil
½	cup chopped butternut squash (½-inch cubes)
½	cup trimmed and finely sliced Brussels sprouts
1	teaspoon unsalted butter
1	tablespoon roughly chopped fresh sage

¼	teaspoon ground allspice
1	teaspoon kosher salt
1	teaspoon sugar
⅓	cup arborio rice
1	cup finely chopped shallots
1	teaspoon finely chopped garlic
⅓	cup dry white wine
¼	cup shredded Parmesan cheese

1 | You will need three pans for this recipe: a large sauté pan for the roasted vegetables, a medium sauté pan for the risotto, and a medium saucepot for the simmering stock and water.

2 | In a medium saucepot, add the water and chicken stock and bring to just under a simmer.

3 | In a large sauté pan over medium heat, add 1½ tablespoons of the olive oil. Once the oil is hot, add the butternut squash and Brussels sprouts. Stir occasionally until evenly golden. Add the butter, sage, allspice, salt, and sugar. Stir and cook for 1 more minute, then turn off the heat. Set aside while you make the rice.

continued

4 | In a medium sauté pan over high heat, add the remaining 2 tablespoons olive oil. Once the oil is hot, add the rice, shallots, and garlic. Stir continuously until the rice starts to look clear on the edges, about 30 seconds. Add the white wine and stir continuously until absorbed. Add the hot water and chicken stock a ladleful at a time, stirring continuously until each addition is absorbed. After 5 ladlesful of stock have been absorbed, start tasting the rice. You want it to be al dente. Continue adding stock and stirring. Make sure the rice stays at a light boil as you stir. Adjust the finished risotto so that it flows nicely on the plate. If it is too thin, you may have to boil the rice for a moment longer or add another ladleful of stock if too thick. Keep in mind that the risotto will thicken as it cools on the plate.

5 | Once the rice is al dente, add a touch more stock so that the rice moves side to side like a slow-moving wave—not solid but not saucy. Stir in the roasted squash and Brussels sprouts. Spoon the risotto onto plates and top with the Parmesan. Enjoy.

FLAVOR SECRETS

Allspice is exactly that—one spice that tastes like all of the great baking spices rolled into one. The sweetness of cinnamon, the earthy holiday spice of nutmeg, the boldness of cloves, and a little black pepper heat. Although typically a baking spice, it's great in savory dishes as well.

WHITE BEAN SOUP WITH ROSEMARY PESTO

This easy, classic soup is smooth and creamy, with the flavor burst of pesto. You can puree it and add more beans for a chunkier soup or eat it as is. This is a healthy, hearty meal unto itself.

SERVES 4

1	tablespoon olive oil
1	tablespoon finely chopped garlic
¼	cup roughly chopped carrots
¼	cup roughly chopped celery
1	cup thinly sliced yellow onions
2	cups chicken stock
One	15-ounce can Bush's Best cannellini beans, rinsed and drained
1	teaspoon kosher salt

PESTO

2	tablespoons fresh rosemary, finely chopped
1	cup fresh flat-leaf parsley
½	cup olive oil
½	teaspoon kosher salt
½	teaspoon ground white pepper
1	tablespoon finely chopped garlic
½	cup grated Parmesan cheese

1 | In a medium pot over medium heat, add the olive oil, garlic, carrots, celery, and onions. Cook, stirring occasionally, until deep golden, about 15 minutes. Add the chicken stock, cannellini, and salt. Bring to a boil. Turn down the heat to low, cover, and cook for 15 minutes. Remove from the heat and let cool.

2 | Transfer the slightly cooled soup to a blender and puree until smooth. (Put a towel over the top of the blender to protect against splattering.) Set aside.

3 | To prepare the pesto, combine the rosemary, parsley, olive oil, salt, pepper, garlic, and Parmesan in a food processor. Pulse-chop until you have a coarse puree.

4 | Ladle the soup into bowls and spoon a few dollops of pesto on top. Serve.

GORGONZOLA, CARAMELIZED PEAR, AND GOAT CHEESE SANDWICH

Gorgonzola is the milder blue cheese cousin of the strong French blue cheese. It is also creamy and richer. It melts into a thick sauce on this grilled cheese sandwich and creates a fantastic flavor contrast with the sweet caramelized pears. While I recommend butter pears (a great texture for this dish), any ripe pear will do—just err on the side of slightly harder pears versus overly ripe ones, so they don't end up mushy after cooking. A loaf of brioche or a handmade loaf of white bread works best for this recipe, but regular sliced sandwich bread is fine if that's your only option.

SERVES 3

2 pears, such as butter pears	6 ounces creamy Gorgonzola, at room temperature
3 tablespoons unsalted butter	Six ½-inch-thick slices white bread
1 teaspoon olive oil	1 cup arugula, plus more for garnish, if desired
½ cup sauvignon blanc	
½ teaspoon kosher salt	

1 | Wash the pears and slice them ¼ inch thick.

2 | In a large sauté pan over medium heat, melt 1 tablespoon of the butter with the olive oil. Add the pear slices and sauté to golden, about 5 minutes. Manage the heat so the pears become evenly golden but not too soft. If the heat is too high, they won't get evenly golden. If the heat is too low, they'll become mushy before they are golden.

3 | Add the white wine and salt and simmer until the liquid is mostly evaporated. Let the wine reduce until it looks like a saucy glaze on the pears. Remember, it will thicken a little when it cools, so allow a little liquid to remain when you stop the cooking. Use a rubber spatula to remove the pears and sauce from the pan. Set aside to cool.

4 | Place the Gorgonzola evenly in little clumps on each of 3 slices of the bread; it can be hard to spread. Lay the pear slices on top of the cheese, and the arugula on top of the pears. Place 1 slice of bread on top of each sandwich and push down to flatten a little.

continued

5 | On a griddle or in a nonstick pan, melt another 1 tablespoon of the remaining butter over medium heat. Lay the sandwiches in the pan and rub them in the butter. Cook until golden. When the sandwiches are golden, add the remaining 1 tablespoon butter to the pan. Flip the sandwiches over and rub them in the butter to evenly coat. Cook until the second side is golden and the cheese is soft.

6 | Slice the sandwiches in triangles and serve on a platter with more arugula (shredded, if preferred) on top as a garnish.

FARFALLE WITH BLACK OLIVES, SHAVED PECORINO, AND LEMON

The shape of farfalle is not just for looks—farfalle's flat "butterfly wings" hold the pieces of black olive and pecorino perfectly in this recipe. One simple squeeze of lemon juice is a flavor boost to many dishes. Here, it heightens the cured flavor of the olives and the saltiness of the pecorino (dry sheep's milk cheese). Taste the sauce before and after you add the lemon to see the difference for yourself. And because the olive oil *is* your sauce here, be sure to use a good one with lots of sharp, green flavor.

SERVES 4 TO 6

One 1-pound box farfalle or pasta of your choice	2 teaspoons finely chopped fresh rosemary
3 tablespoons extra virgin olive oil	5 tablespoons fresh lemon juice
½ cup oil-cured black olives, pitted and chopped in half	¼ cup heavy cream
2 tablespoons finely chopped garlic	¾ cup shaved pecorino cheese
⅛ teaspoon chile flakes	3 tablespoons chopped fresh flat-leaf parsley

1 | Bring a large pot of water to a boil. Once the water is boiling, add enough salt to make the water a little salty, about ¼ cup. This helps bring out the full flavor of the pasta. Add the farfalle to the boiling water. While the pasta is boiling, make the sauce.

2 | In a large skillet over medium heat, add the olive oil. Once the oil is hot, add the olives, garlic, chile flakes, and rosemary and cook just until the garlic and rosemary become fragrant. Add the lemon juice and simmer for 30 seconds. Stir in the cream and simmer for 1 minute, then remove from the heat.

3 | Turn off the heat if the pasta is not al dente (still firm in the middle; don't be afraid to taste a piece instead of relying on a timer). As soon as it is ready, drain the pasta (but never rinse; another secret). Save a touch of the cooking water.

4 | Place the pasta in the skillet of sauce on the stove top and turn the heat to medium-high. Stir to coat evenly. Boil the pasta in the sauce for 1 minute, adding the reserved pasta water if it is too dry. This allows the pasta to absorb the sauce. This sauce is meant to coat the pasta lightly but not be overly saucy. Don't worry that you don't have enough sauce. You do. :)

5 | Place the pasta on serving plates and top with the pecorino and parsley. Serve immediately.

FLAVOR SECRETS

Making perfect pasta is easy. Add salt—but not oil—to your water. (Salt pulls out the flavor of your pasta; oil simply coats it and keeps flavors from sticking to it.) Use 1 gallon of water or three times the amount of pasta you have. Make sure the water is boiling rapidly. After dropping the pasta into the water, stir the pasta a couple of times while it cooks. Drain when al dente (and don't be afraid to taste a piece or two to be sure it's right).

OPEN-FACE LASAGNA WITH MOREL MUSHROOMS AND ASPARAGUS

In this recipe, which is quicker to prepare than traditional lasagna, you get the rich, sweet goodness of tomatoes, the heat of chile, and the earthy vegetable heft of mushrooms and asparagus—a beautiful medley of flavor contrasts.

SERVES 4

1½	pounds wild or morel mushrooms, or mushrooms of your choice
¼	cup olive oil, plus more for drizzling
½	teaspoon kosher salt
½	teaspoon freshly ground black pepper
	Pinch of chile flakes
½	cup shallots, finely chopped
16	asparagus spears, trimmed and cut into 2-inch pieces
1	tablespoon finely chopped garlic
1	cup dry white wine
1	tablespoon unsalted butter
4	lasagna sheets
12	ounces Taleggio or triple cream cow's milk cheese of your choice
2	ounces Parmesan cheese, grated, plus more for garnish
½	cup fresh basil, shredded

1 | Rinse off the mushrooms and pat dry. Cut off the thickest part of the stems and discard. Cut the mushrooms into 1-inch pieces, roughly halves or quarters, depending on the size of the mushrooms.

2 | In a large, wide skillet over medium-high heat, add the olive oil. Once the oil is hot, add the mushrooms, salt, pepper, and chile flakes. Stir to coat the mushrooms evenly with the olive oil. Sauté until the mushrooms become golden, 12 to 15 minutes. Add the shallots and asparagus, stir, and cook until the mushrooms are deep golden and the asparagus is tender but firm, about 8 more minutes. Stir in the garlic and cook for 30 seconds more, just to bring out the flavor of the garlic but not to brown it.

3 | Add the white wine and simmer until reduced by half. Turn off the heat and set aside. Stir in the butter until melted and fully incorporated.

4 | While the mushrooms are cooking, bring a large pot of water to a boil. Once the water is boiling, cook the lasagna according to the package instructions. Once the pasta is cooked to al dente, pull it out of the water and drain (do not rinse). Rub with a touch of olive oil to prevent sticking and set 1 sheet of pasta on each of four plates.

5 | Divide the Taleggio and Parmesan evenly across the pasta. Spoon the mushroom-asparagus mixture over the cheeses. The heat will partially melt the cheeses. Shower the basil on top of each plate. Drizzle a touch of extra virgin olive oil and a touch more Parmesan over each. Serve.

FUSILLI WITH FENNEL SEED—OREGANO CHICKEN, MUSHROOMS, AND CREAM SAUCE

I have many delicious memories of mushrooms in cream sauce—the base for so many of my mom's dishes. Freshly ground fennel seed is the key to this dish, giving it a bright, almost citrusy note that is further enhanced by the oregano. It's important to have your mushrooms, shallots, and garlic ready to add to these herbs at the right time, so that you don't burn the fennel seeds and bits in the pan. This is creamy comfort food at its best.

SERVES 4

¼ teaspoon kosher salt, plus more for seasoning	¾ box (12 ounces) fusilli or pasta of your choice
One 8-ounce skinless, boneless chicken breast (or chicken thighs for more tender meat)	2 cups thinly sliced mushrooms
	½ cup shallots, finely chopped
	1 teaspoon finely chopped garlic
¼ teaspoon freshly ground black pepper, plus more for seasoning	½ cup heavy cream
1 tablespoon olive oil	1½ cups chicken stock
1 teaspoon fennel seed, roughly ground	6 sun-dried tomatoes, cut into thirds
	4 tablespoons grated Parmesan cheese
1 tablespoon fresh oregano, finely chopped	3 tablespoons roughly chopped fresh flat-leaf parsley

1 | Bring a large pot of water to a boil with enough salt so you can taste it, about ¼ cup.

2 | Cut the chicken into ½-inch slices and then cut the slices in half. Pat dry with a paper towel and season with salt and pepper.

3 | In a large sauté pan over medium-high heat, add the olive oil. Once the oil is hot, add the chicken and cook until golden, about 3 minutes. Add the fennel seed and oregano and stir. When the fennel and oregano are toasted (you will smell it after about 2 minutes), remove from the heat. Remove the chicken from the pan and set aside. (The chicken will not be fully cooked at this point. It will finish cooking in the sauce later.)

4 | Add the fusilli to the boiling water and cook according to the package instructions.

5 | While the pasta is cooking, add the mushrooms, shallots, and garlic to the pan with the fennel and oregano. Turn to medium heat and scrape the bottom of the pan as you stir. Cook until deep golden and soft, about 10 minutes. Manage the heat and be ready to turn it down if necessary. The goal is to layer and build the flavor of the ingredients in the bottom of the pan but without burning them.

6 | Add the cream, stir, and cook for 1 minute. Add the chicken stock, ¼ teaspoon salt, and ¼ teaspoon pepper and simmer until boiled down by about one-third. You want a saucy consistency. You also want enough sauce to evenly coat the pasta without being dry or too wet. Add the reserved chicken and the sun-dried tomatoes. Turn off the heat if pasta is not ready.

7 | When the pasta is al dente, strain, saving ¼ cup of the pasta water, and add the pasta to the pan with the sauce. Simmer for 1 minute while stirring, allowing the pasta to absorb the sauce. If the sauce gets too thick, use some of the reserved pasta water to thin it out. Stir in the Parmesan.

8 | Remove from the heat and serve immediately, garnished with the parsley.

PORK CHOPS WITH CARAMELIZED APPLES AND ARUGULA

In this gourmet version of the classic combination of pork chops and applesauce, fresh apple juice and rosemary create a sweet glaze for the tender chops.

SERVES 2

2	pork chops
	Salt and freshly ground black pepper to taste
2	tablespoons olive oil
1	cup finely chopped shallots
1	medium green apple, cut into ½-inch cubes
1	garlic clove, chopped

½	cup brandy
1	cup apple juice (ideally fresh)
2	teaspoons fresh rosemary, finely chopped
1	cup chicken stock
1	tablespoon unsalted butter
2	cups arugula, washed and dried

1 | For maximum juiciness, brine the pork chops for 4 hours if you can (see Flavor Secrets, below). Pat the pork chops dry with a paper towel and season with salt and pepper.

2 | In a sauté pan over medium-high heat, add the olive oil. Heat the oil until it just starts to haze. Add the pork chops and sauté until golden on both sides, about 3 minutes per side. Closely monitor the heat so the pork chops get a deep golden brown but so the bits at the bottom of the pan don't burn—they are the flavor foundation for your sauce. Remove the pork chops and set aside.

3 | Add the shallots, apples, and garlic to the same pan. Cook for 2 minutes or until golden. Use tongs to scrape the bits off the bottom of the pan. Add the brandy and let boil, reducing the liquid by half. Add the apple juice and rosemary, and boil for 1 minute. Add the chicken stock and boil (reduce) until you have a nice saucy consistency. Add the butter. Turn off the heat and stir just until the butter is melted. Stir in the arugula.

4 | Place each pork chop on a plate. Pour the sauce with the arugula over the top.

FLAVOR SECRETS

To prepare a brine, combine 1 cup water, ¼ cup kosher salt, and ¼ cup brown sugar. Bring to a boil for 1 minute to dissolve the salt and sugar. Remove from the heat and cool. Stir in 3 cups cold water. Submerge the meat in the brine for at least 4 hours.

PENNE BOLOGNESE

If you like meat and pasta, a good Bolognese is an unbeatable combination. It's the essence of meat, without the knife. This recipe is all about the richness of meat browned over high heat, the layers of aromatic rosemary and thyme, the crispness of white wine, and the finishing touch of nutty, rich Parmesan. Although penne is recommended, feel free to choose the pasta for your mood. A wedge of fresh crusty bread is essential for mopping up the sauce on your plate. And this pairs perfectly with a glass of great Sangiovese, Barbera, or your favorite full-bodied red wine.

SERVES 6

¼	cup olive oil	2	cups tomato paste
¼	cup finely chopped garlic	2½	cups whole milk
2	cups finely diced yellow onions	1	cup dry white wine
½	cup shredded carrots	1	tablespoon finely chopped fresh thyme
½	cup finely chopped celery	1	teaspoon finely chopped fresh rosemary
¾	pound ground beef (15% fat)	One	1-pound box penne
¾	pound ground pork	2	tablespoons unsalted butter
1	tablespoon kosher salt	⅓	cup grated Parmesan cheese
½	teaspoon freshly ground black pepper	¼	cup fresh flat-leaf parsley, finely chopped

1 | In a large, wide, shallow pot over medium-high heat, add the olive oil. (A large, wide pot is important to develop good color. If the pot is too narrow and deep, everything boils instead of browns.) Add the garlic, onions, carrots, and celery. Cook, stirring occasionally, until golden, about 10 minutes. Monitor the heat and be careful not to burn the garlic.

2 | Add the ground beef and ground pork and break apart into small pieces. Season with the salt and pepper. Cook over medium-high heat until evenly dark brown, about 40 minutes. Continue to adjust the heat down as the meat browns so that it does not burn on the bottom as the moisture leaves. Stir and scrape the bottom of the pan with a metal spoon every 10 minutes.

3 | Add the tomato paste and stir to combine evenly. Cook until it is a deep, dark reddish brown, about 20 minutes. Keep turning down the heat as needed to avoid burning. Scrape the bottom of the pot often with a metal spoon and stir to incorporate the flavor. Color equals flavor, so make sure you get the meat dark brown and the garlic, onions, carrots, and celery nice and golden. Let the tomato paste get really dark before you add the milk below. When you think it's ready, wait another 15 minutes. Once you add the milk, the color and flavor will come together perfectly.

4 | Stir in the milk and scrape the bottom to incorporate fully. Cover the pot about 80 percent closed to avoid splattering and prevent too much reduction. Once the mixture comes to a boil, turn down the heat to very low and cook for 15 minutes. It will have a thick, saucy consistency.

5 | Bring a pot of water large enough to hold the pasta to a boil and add ¼ cup kosher salt.

6 | Meanwhile, add the white wine, thyme, and rosemary to the sauce. Stir and allow the sauce to come to a boil. Turn down the heat to very low and cover the pot 80 percent closed. Cook for 15 minutes. (This will concentrate the wine flavor while removing most of the alcohol.)

7 | While the sauce is in the final stage of cooking, add the penne to the boiling water, stir once, and cook according to the package instructions.

8 | When the penne is al dente, drain but keep about 1 cup of the cooking water. Put the penne into the meat sauce and simmer for 1 minute so that the pasta and the sauce become one. If the sauce is too thick, stir in some of the reserved pasta water. Turn off the heat and stir in the butter and Parmesan.

9 | Divide the pasta among six plates and sprinkle with the parsley. Serve immediately.

OSSO BUCCO

Osso bucco is the epitome of great stewed meat. It's essentially veal shank seared to golden, then bathed in a rich tomato broth and cooked low and slow until if falls off the bone, rich with marrow. (On one of our first dates, I watched my future wife passionately yet with surgical precision remove every last bite of marrow with a wine corkscrew—the woman of my dreams!) Veal shank is not cheap, so make this when you want a special, unforgettable meal, and pair it with creamy polenta, orzo, or saffron risotto. This recipe yields a lot more sauce than you'll likely serve—the extra works deliciously on top of pasta the next day.

SERVES 4

5	large veal shanks
1	tablespoon kosher salt, plus more for seasoning
	Freshly ground black pepper
1	cup all-purpose flour
3	tablespoons olive oil
2	tablespoons unsalted butter
1	cup finely diced yellow onions
½	cup finely diced celery
½	cup finely diced carrots
2	tablespoons finely chopped garlic
2	cups dry white wine

One	28-ounce can whole plum tomatoes, pureed
3	cups chicken stock
2	teaspoons finely chopped fresh rosemary
1	tablespoon fresh oregano, finely chopped

GREMOLATA

2	garlic cloves
¼	cup fresh flat-leaf parsley
	Zest of 1 lemon

1 | Preheat the oven to 300°F.

2 | Pat the veal shanks dry with a paper towel and season them liberally with salt and pepper. Lay the flour evenly on a plate and coat each shank in flour, shaking off the excess. Place a shallow pot with a tight-fitting, ovenproof lid over medium heat and add the olive oil. Set each shank in the hot olive oil and sauté until golden on both sides, about 4 minutes per side. Make sure the veal is golden brown on both sides before removing it from the initial sauté. That's where a lot of the flavor develops. Remove from the oil and set aside.

3 | To the same pan, add the butter, onions, celery, carrots, and garlic and sauté over medium heat until golden, about 4 minutes. Add the white wine and simmer until reduced by half. (This removes the alcohol and concentrates the flavor of the wine.)

4 | Add the pureed tomatoes, chicken stock, 1 tablespoon kosher salt, rosemary, and oregano and bring to a boil. Remove from the heat and add the veal shanks to the sauce. Cover the pan tightly and bake in the oven for 3½ hours, or until the meat is falling off the bone. Carefully remove the meat (keeping it intact on the bone) and set aside.

5 | Place the pot with the sauce on the stove over medium heat and let the sauce boil, reducing it to a light sauce consistency—not thick but not watery. You will have more sauce than you need, but it is necessary to properly cook the veal.

6 | While the sauce is reducing, prepare the gremolata. Mix the garlic, parsley, and lemon zest on a cutting board and chop finely.

7 | Divide the veal among serving plates and spoon the sauce on top. Sprinkle with the gremolata and serve.

FLAVOR SECRETS

A classic Italian finishing condiment, gremolata is a mixture of lemon zest, parsley, and garlic. The moment it hits the hot osso bucco, it releases a perfume of citrus, fresh herbs, and the mild heat of the garlic. Gremolata adds lightness and brightness to hearty stewed meat and can wake up a simple piece of leftover chicken. A tiny touch creates a huge burst of flavor.

JOIE DE VIVRE
FRANCE

...

HERBES DE PROVENCE, OVEN-DRIED TOMATO, AND GOAT CHEESE TARTINE 76

SALADE NIÇOISE WITH HERBES DE PROVENCE VINAIGRETTE 77

ORANGE—PICKLED FENNEL SALAD WITH BLACK OLIVES
AND TOASTED FENNEL SEED 79

ENDIVE, RADISH, AND FENNEL SALAD WITH ANCHOVY VINAIGRETTE 80

BOUILLABAISSE 83

TWO-PORK CROQUE MONSIEUR WITH SPICED MORNAY 86

TEN-MINUTE PAN QUICHE 88

STEAMED CURRIED MUSSELS 89

BLACK PEPPER DUCK WITH CRISPY SHREDS AND SPICY CHERRY CHUTNEY 90

WHITE PEPPER CASSOULET 92

STRIP STEAK WITH "SECRET" GREEN SAUCE 94

BEEF BOURGUIGNON 95

France is the indisputable epicenter of haute cuisine. It's the birthplace of countless classics, from Champagne, foie gras, and *pommes frites* to cassoulet, quiche, and croissants. France has brought us the Cordon Bleu, wine appellations, *Michelin* guides, hundreds of cooking techniques that have been around for centuries, and so many different types of cheese that Charles de Gaulle, former president of France, once lamented, "How can anyone govern a nation that has two hundred and forty-six different kinds of cheeses?" In fact, it was cheese—to be specific, the huge pleasure of eating my first croque madame in Paris (the joys of which you'll find on page 197)—that turned me on to the marvels of French cuisine and its buttery, herbal flavor profiles.

That said, French cuisine is more than the sum of its parts. People of different ethnicities have crossed France's borders for centuries and influenced its cuisine, so it's no wonder that in Paris I also discovered North African harissa and *pho,* the sensational Vietnamese soup. The recipes here are but a few of the many French classics I adore, but with my globally influenced spin. *Bon appétit!*

BLACK PEPPER

HERBES DE PROVENCE

SAFFRON

TARRAGON

BLACK PEPPER—the simple black peppercorns we all know and love—enlivens so many French dishes. You can release its potent, spicy fresh flavor simply by twisting your pepper grinder. Black pepper balances flavor in a dish and binds with salt to create an incredible crust on meat. Ground fresh and used in volume, it actually becomes spicy and is completely different from its dry, flat, pre-ground form.

HERBES DE PROVENCE is an illustrious herbal blend that represents the best of southern France's fragrant countryside—a combination of woody summer aromatics that are used fresh in the summer and then dried the rest of the year. Although ingredients can vary, herbes de Provence usually consists of thyme, rosemary, marjoram, oregano, sage, savory, and lavender. (I prefer blends with less lavender, which can often overpower the other herbs.) Herbes de Provence can be used as a seasoning or a rub before grilling fish, poultry, and meats, or added to a light vinaigrette.

SAFFRON See page 29.

TARRAGON is like the traveled cousin of mint, with anise and citrus tones. It's that unique taste you get in béarnaise sauce, and it loves taking a bath in tomato broth with seafood or accenting a seared steak. I don't recommend it dried as it loses most of its charm.

FRENCH FLAVOR FAMILY

HERBES DE PROVENCE, OVEN-DRIED TOMATO, AND GOAT CHEESE TARTINE

Herbes de Provence smells like summer in France. Here it comes together with the buttery goodness of goat cheese, the sweet tang of tomato, and the doughy crunch of bread. You'll want to use the best bread you can find. Artisan bread—thick crust, big pores, with a chewy interior—is a richer eating experience than using thin packaged bread, which can get soggy and won't hold up to the toppings. Eat this tartine tapas style or as a small meal unto itself.

SERVES 4

4 thick slices rustic bread	¾ cup creamy goat cheese
2 tablespoons extra virgin olive oil	2 tablespoons roughly chopped fresh flat-leaf parsley (optional)
24 oven-dried tomato slices	¼ cup roughly chopped pitted olives (optional)
1 tablespoon herbes de Provence	

1 | Preheat the broiler.

2 | Lay out the bread on a sheet pan. Drizzle the bread with the olive oil. Place on the top rack of the oven and broil until slightly golden. Remove from the oven but do not turn off the broiler.

3 | Lay the dried tomato slices evenly over the bread. Sprinkle evenly with the herbes de Provence.

4 | Dollop the goat cheese over the tomatoes. Place the sheet pan back under the broiler for about 1 minute, or until the goat cheese softens and becomes a touch golden.

5 | Serve one tartine per plate or cut them into thirds and place on a platter as appetizers. Garnish with the chopped parsley and black olives for a nice presentation.

FLAVOR SECRETS

If you don't have oven-dried tomatoes, you can rub the bread with a ripe tomato or top the bread with a chopped-up canned tomato. This is more like the *Pan y Tomate* Tapas (page 102).

SALADE NIÇOISE WITH HERBES DE PROVENCE VINAIGRETTE

There's no other salad that speaks French more perfectly than the salade Niçoise. Originating in Nice (hence it's name), this healthy, bright salad was introduced to America by none other than Julia Child. Salade Niçoise is a medley of crisp lettuce and green beans, hard-cooked eggs and black olives, all crowned by tuna and anchovies. The black olive herbes de Provence dressing is my spin on this French classic, which goes splendidly with a slice of grilled or toasted rustic bread.

SERVES 4

VINAIGRETTE

- ¼ cup oil-cured black olives, pitted
- 1 teaspoon herbes de Provence
- ¼ cup red wine vinegar
- ½ cup olive oil
- 1 teaspoon Dijon mustard

SALAD

- 2 cups haricots verts (French green beans)
- 2 large hard-cooked eggs, cooled
- 12 baby red potatoes, boiled and cooled
- One 12-ounce piece ahi tuna or two 6-ounce cans tuna of your choice
- 2 teaspoons olive oil
- Pinch of kosher salt and freshly ground black pepper
- 8 quarts mixed greens, rinsed and dried

1 | First, prepare the vinaigrette. In a food processor, puree the olives, herbes de Provence, vinegar, olive oil, and mustard. Stop when the dressing comes together but the olives are still in small pieces. Set aside. (You can make and refrigerate this dressing as many as 3 days ahead of time.)

2 | For the salad, fill a large pot with water, place it over high heat, and bring to a boil. Drop in the green beans and boil for 2 minutes. Fill a medium bowl with ice water. Drain the beans and drop them into the ice water, stirring them vigorously to cool quickly. Once they are cool, drain the beans again, pat them dry with a paper towel, and set aside.

3 | Cut the hard-cooked eggs into slices. Cut the potatoes into quarters. They should be fork-tender but solid, not mushy.

continued

4 | Cut the tuna into four equal-size pieces. In a medium nonstick pan over medium-high heat, add the olive oil. Pat the tuna dry with a paper towel and season with salt and pepper. Place in the pan and sear until deep golden. I like to leave the tuna medium-rare (about 2 minutes on the first side and 1 minute on the second side). Flip and repeat until the tuna reaches your desired doneness. Set aside to come to room temperature.

5 | Once all of the ingredients are sufficiently cooled, in a large salad or mixing bowl, add the salad greens, green beans, sliced eggs, and potatoes. Drizzle the vinaigrette over the salad. Toss with tongs to evenly coat. It is OK if the eggs break apart—this is a rustic presentation.

6 | Divide the salad among four plates. Lay one slice of tuna on top of each plate and serve.

FLAVOR SECRETS

Hard cooking eggs versus hard boiling gives you more flavor and prevents the green ring from forming around the yolk. To hard-cook, place an even layer of eggs on the bottom of a pot. Cover the eggs with cold water by about 1 inch. Heat over high heat until the water comes to boil. Immediately remove the pot from the heat and cover. Let the eggs sit in the hot water for about 11 minutes if they are medium size. Drain and serve warm, or cool under running cold water or in an ice bath.

ORANGE—PICKLED FENNEL SALAD WITH BLACK OLIVES AND TOASTED FENNEL SEED

Fresh fennel is often overlooked in America, but it's frequently found on French dinner tables. Crisp and crunchy, fennel has a grassy, dill-like back note that contrasts perfectly with the sweet, citrusy orange, and it adds wonderful textures and little bursts of subtle licorice flavor as well. Together, orange and fennel, two lovely partners, create a clean, refreshing salad.

SERVES 4

3 cups thinly sliced fennel	½ cup fresh orange juice
2 tablespoons fresh mint, chopped in large pieces	½ teaspoon fennel seed, toasted and ground to a coarse texture
⅓ cup roughly chopped pitted green olives	½ teaspoon kosher salt

In a wide bowl, mix the fennel, mint, olives, orange juice, ground fennel seed, and salt together. Let sit at room temperature for 20 minutes or in the refrigerator for up to 24 hours. Serve on plates as a side salad or appetizer.

ENDIVE, RADISH, AND FENNEL SALAD WITH ANCHOVY VINAIGRETTE

The peppery bite of radishes and the bright licorice crunch of fennel ignite the endive in this salad. The vinaigrette is light yet full of flavor, infused with the sharp sweetness of shallots and the subtle umami of anchovy—a perfect beginning to osso bucco or another heavy meat course.

SERVES 4

¼ cup fresh lemon juice, plus a squeeze to taste	¾ teaspoon kosher salt
2 tablespoons finely chopped shallots	1 cup thinly sliced radishes
1 teaspoon Dijon mustard	3 cups thinly sliced fennel
1 teaspoon anchovy paste	3 cups thinly sliced endive
½ cup olive oil	½ cup shaved Parmesan cheese

1 | In a food processor, puree the lemon juice, shallots, mustard, anchovy paste, olive oil, and ¼ teaspoon of the salt until smooth. Strain, pressing all the liquid out. Discard the solids.

2 | In a small bowl, toss the radishes and fennel with the remaining ½ teaspoon salt and the squeeze of lemon juice. Make sure the radishes and fennel are cut thin and lay fairly flat in the marinade so that they marinate evenly. Let sit for 15 minutes.

3 | In a large bowl, toss together the radishes, fennel, and endive. Using tongs, mix with some of the vinaigrette and taste. Evenly coat the endive.

4 | Divide among four plates, garnish with the Parmesan, and serve.

BOUILLABAISSE

Monkfish, black cod, Florida rock shrimp, mussels, sea scallops—any kind of fresh seafood works in this classic French stew and creates rich flavor contrasts and textures. You simply can't go wrong with bouillabaisse, especially when served with a slice of bread and a killer glass of dry white wine.

SERVES 4

8	medium shrimp
One	12-ounce piece cod, striped bass, or preferred whitefish fillet (boneless and skinless)
1	teaspoon kosher salt, plus more for seasoning
	Freshly ground black pepper
1	pound black mussels
3	tablespoons olive oil
1	cup finely chopped shallots
1	cup thinly sliced red bell pepper (2-inch strips)

2	tablespoons chopped garlic
1	cup dry white wine
3	cups fish broth or water
2	cups canned plum tomatoes or tomato sauce (without added seasoning)
1	teaspoon saffron threads or powder
1	cup cubed fingerling or russet potatoes (½-inch cubes)
¼	cup roughly chopped fresh flat-leaf parsley

1 | Peel the shrimp, cut out the vein along the back, and save the shells. (Skip this step if you're using pre-shelled shrimp.) Pat the shrimp and fish fillet dry with a paper towel. Season with salt and black pepper.

2 | Pull the beards off the mussels by sliding them to the end of the shell and pulling. (Sometimes the mussels are already clean.) Rinse them off and let drain.

3 | In a wide shallow pot over medium-high heat, add 2 tablespoons of the olive oil. Once the oil is hot, add the shrimp and fish without crowding. Cook until golden, about 1 minute for the shrimp and 3 minutes for the fish. The shrimp are done when they go from translucent to opaque. The moment you see them change, take them out. Flip over the fish and cook until almost done but still a little undercooked (it will finish cooking in the broth). Remove from the pot and set aside on a plate.

continued

4 | Add the remaining 1 tablespoon olive oil to the pot and add the shallots, bell peppers, and garlic. Sauté in the pot for 2 minutes, until golden. Add the mussels and cook until they just start to open, about 2 minutes. Add the white wine and simmer until reduced by half and the mussels are fully open, about 4 minutes. Remove the mussels with tongs and add to the plate of cooked fish. Remember to always discard any mussels or clams that do not open after being cooked.

5 | To the same pot, add the fish broth, shrimp shells (if you have them), tomatoes, saffron, and 1 teaspoon salt and bring to a boil. Turn off the heat and allow to cool until you are comfortable pouring it into a blender. Puree the mixture in a blender until smooth. Strain through a mesh strainer back into the pot and discard the solids.

6 | Add the potatoes and bring to just under a simmer. Cover the pot and cook until the potatoes are tender. Add the cooked shrimp, fish, and mussels to the pot and turn off the heat. Don't boil the fish or it will get tough. Stir to break up the fish into chunks. The residual heat of the broth will finish cooking the fish and shrimp. Taste one to be sure.

7 | Ladle equal amounts of broth and seafood into each of four bowls. Garnish with the parsley and serve.

FLAVOR SECRETS

Leave out the saffron and use ¼ cup fresh tarragon leaves for a layer of deep, citrusy flavor.

TWO-PORK CROQUE MONSIEUR WITH SPICED MORNAY

No one knows where Mornay sauce comes from, or which Duc de Mornay, if any, is responsible for this almost scandalously voluptuous and creamy cheese-based sauce. All we know is that it's so simple and insanely delicious. My version of croque monsieur includes smoky bacon and herbes de Provence, with a quick version of Mornay—not for dieters! Serve with a small salad.

SERVES 4

8	slices bacon	1	cup milk
2	tablespoons unsalted butter	¾	cup grated Gruyère cheese
1	tablespoon herbes de Provence	1	teaspoon fresh lemon juice
1	teaspoon freshly ground black pepper, plus more for seasoning	8	slices rustic, porous white bread
1	tablespoon all-purpose flour	8	thin slices boiled ham, at room temperature

1 | Cook the bacon to golden and set aside to drain on a paper towel.

2 | To make the sauce, in a small pot over medium heat, melt the butter. Add the herbes de Provence and pepper. Stir just for a moment to allow the herbs to infuse into the butter. Whisk in the flour a little at a time. Stir rapidly with the whisk to incorporate all the flour. Once the mixture is smooth, slowly add the milk, whisking continuously, and bring to a boil. Turn down the heat to a simmer and cook for 1 minute. Taste (blow hard to cool first) and make sure the raw flour flavor is gone. If it isn't, continue to simmer and stir for 1 minute. Remove from the heat. Stir in ¼ cup of the Gruyère and the lemon juice. Set aside.

3 | Preheat the broiler.

4 | Toast the bread in the toaster to a light golden. Lay 4 pieces of the bread on a sheet pan. Add 2 slices of ham, then 2 slices of bacon to each. Spoon one-quarter of the Mornay sauce onto each. It is OK (and desirable) for the sauce to run out a little bit. Place the remaining slices of bread on top of the sauce. Divide the remainder of the Gruyère among the tops of the sandwiches. Sprinkle a little more pepper on top of each sandwich and place under the broiler. Broil until the cheese is golden.

TEN-MINUTE PAN QUICHE

A French classic from the Lorraine region, quiche is the world's favorite oven-baked egg-and-cheese dish. This quick, easy version replicates the classic in a fraction of the time. Whether or not you make your own bread crumbs by grinding up garlic croutons or day-old bread, the bread crumbs will toast up nicely, creating the "crust," and the fillings are unlimited. (I love feta cheese, black olives, and fresh mint.) This is a fun recipe to make with kids because they can create their own quiches using whatever fillings they like.

SERVES 2

4	large eggs	1	cup bread crumbs
¼	cup water	1	teaspoon herbes de Provence
¼	teaspoon kosher salt	¼	cup roughly chopped tomatoes
1	tablespoon olive oil	¼	cup chopped spinach leaves

1 | In a medium bowl, whisk together the eggs, water, and salt. Set aside.

2 | In a medium nonstick skillet over medium heat, add the olive oil. Make sure it is evenly spread out on the bottom and sides of the pan. Once the olive oil is hot, add the bread crumbs and herbes de Provence and stir. Using a rubber spatula, press down firmly to form a "crust" in the bottom and up the sides of the pan. Make sure to monitor the heat. If it's too high, the crust may burn before the egg sets. If it's too low, the egg will set without a nice golden crust. (Smell just above the pan. If there's an overly toasty smell before the egg is set, the heat may be too high.)

3 | Carefully spread the tomatoes and spinach across the crust. Gently pour in the whisked eggs. Cover the pan and turn down the heat a touch. Cook until the egg is set but still moist looking, about 10 minutes. Uncover and remove from the heat.

4 | Using a rubber spatula, divide the quiche in half and slide each half out and onto a plate. Serve as is or with a mixed green salad.

STEAMED CURRIED MUSSELS

This perennial French favorite delivers the fresh, briny juice of mussels and the mouthwatering combo of white wine, butter, and shallots. Serve with plenty of toasted rustic bread to dip into the sauce.

SERVES 2

1 pound black mussels	1½ teaspoons ground turmeric
1 tablespoon canola oil	¼ teaspoon chile flakes
¼ cup finely chopped shallots	½ cup dry white wine
1 teaspoon roughly chopped garlic	⅓ cup coconut milk
½ teaspoon cumin seed, toasted and ground	Pinch of kosher salt
½ teaspoon coriander seed, toasted and ground	1 teaspoon unsalted butter
	2 tablespoons roughly chopped fresh cilantro

1 | Remove beards of the mussels if necessary. The beard looks like a thin string hanging out of the shell; pull it to the end of the mussel and against the end of the shell to remove. Rinse off the mussels and set aside to dry.

2 | In a large, wide pan with high sides or a wok over medium-high heat, add the canola oil. Once the oil is hot, add the shallots and garlic. Cook just until you can smell the garlic, about 30 seconds. Add the cumin, coriander, turmeric, and chile flakes. Toast for 30 seconds. Add the mussels and stir. Cook for 1 minute.

3 | Add the white wine and simmer until the wine is reduced by half. Add the coconut milk and reduce by half. At this point the mussels should be open. If not, turn down the heat and cook until they are. Discard any mussels that don't open. Turn off the heat. Add the salt and stir in the butter until melted.

4 | Serve on a platter or in a wide bowl and garnish with the cilantro. Set out a couple of empty bowls for people to put their mussel shells into.

FLAVOR SECRETS

An unoaked wine such as sauvignon blanc works best in this dish.

BLACK PEPPER DUCK WITH CRISPY SHREDS AND SPICY CHERRY CHUTNEY

Like many of our favorite foods, duck confit was born out of the necessity to preserve food. In this quintessentially French dish, duck legs were cured with salt and then poached in their own fat—giving them a longer shelf life. Here I offer a faster version of juicy, crispy duck with a twist: a sweet and tart chutney. A great middle course or appetizer.

SERVES 4

4 duck legs

½ teaspoon kosher salt, plus more for seasoning

¾ teaspoon freshly ground black pepper, plus more for seasoning

1½ tablespoons olive oil

¼ cup finely chopped shallots

1 teaspoon finely chopped garlic

½ cup dried red cherries, roughly chopped

½ cup red wine vinegar

¼ cup sugar

1 teaspoon dried thyme

1 tablespoon thinly sliced fresh mint

1 | Preheat the oven to 350°F.

2 | Pat the duck dry with a paper towel and season with salt and pepper.

3 | In a medium ovenproof skillet over medium-high heat, add 1 tablespoon of the olive oil. The skillet should be just large enough to fit the duck legs with a little space in between them. This way the fat will gather, and the duck will be moist and juicy instead of the fat spreading out thin and burning on the bottom of the skillet. Once the oil is hot, add the duck, skin side down. Cook until golden, about 3 minutes. Flip over the duck and then transfer the skillet to the oven. Cook until the duck is slightly pink, about 8 minutes. Don't hesitate to cut into it to check.

4 | While the duck is cooking, prepare the chutney. (The chutney can also be made separately ahead as it keeps in the refrigerator for 2 weeks.) In a small, narrow, deep saucepan over medium heat, add the remaining ½ tablespoon olive oil. (A wide, shallow pan can dry out the chutney while it's cooking.) Once the oil is hot, add the shallots and garlic and cook, stirring occasionally, for about 3 minutes, until soft and golden. Add the cherries, vinegar, sugar, thyme, ½ teaspoon salt, and ¾ teaspoon pepper. Turn the heat to a light simmer and cook for 3 minutes, until the mixture reaches a saucy consistency. Turn off the heat and set aside. Keep in mind that the chutney thickens as it cools.

5 | When the duck is done, set aside to cool. Once it is cool, cut the meat off the bone. Use a fork to shred the meat stuck to the bone. Discard the bones. Cut the meat into thin pieces. Pour off and discard the excess fat from the skillet that the duck cooked in and place the skillet over high heat. Once the skillet is hot, add the shredded duck and cook just until crispy—about 2 minutes. Remove from the heat immediately.

6 | Spread the chutney in a thin layer on plates (or a serving platter) and spoon the duck over the chutney. Garnish with the mint and enjoy!

WHITE PEPPER CASSOULET

Cassoulet is France's ultimate warm-your-soul comfort food. Choose the meat you want (except beef), and the herbs and spices you love most, and as long as you follow the basics, the cassoulet will turn out great every time. Instead of oven-dried tomatoes, you can sauté tomatoes with a touch of olive oil in a skillet or cut up a few canned whole tomatoes. Either way, they'll pair excellently with the beans, which not only absorb the flavor of all the meat and herbs, but also serve as a natural thickener to create a rich, savory stew.

SERVES 6 TO 8

1	large head garlic
1	tablespoon olive oil, plus more for drizzling
One	9-ounce Italian sausage or sausage of your choice
One	6-ounce duck breast
One	12-ounce bone-in pork loin chop
1	teaspoon kosher salt, plus more for seasoning
	Freshly ground black pepper
½	cup finely chopped shallots
¼	cup finely chopped carrots
¼	cup finely chopped celery
1½	teaspoons white peppercorns, ground

¼	teaspoon ground allspice
4	cups chicken stock
Three	15-ounce cans Bush's Best cannellini, rinsed and drained
1	teaspoon dried thyme
1	tablespoon herbes de Provence
½	cup roughly chopped oven-dried tomatoes

BREAD CRUMB TOPPING

2	cups bread cubes
¼	cup roughly chopped fresh flat-leaf parsley
1	tablespoon olive oil

1 | Preheat the oven to 400°F.

2 | Cut ¼ inch off the pointed end of the garlic head and set the head on a large piece of aluminum foil, cut side up. Drizzle with a touch of olive oil. Pull the four corners of the foil up to a point to create a sealed pouch for the garlic. Do not press the foil against the garlic or it will stick. Place in the oven and roast for 45 minutes, or until dark brown and soft. Set aside to cool. (This can be done as many as 3 days ahead.)

3 | Dry off the sausage, duck, and pork loin with a paper towel and cut them into ¾-inch pieces, saving the pork bone. Season with salt and pepper and mix together.

4 | In a wide, thick-bottomed, ovenproof pot over medium-high heat, add 1 tablespoon olive oil. Once the oil is hot (almost smoking), add the sausage, duck, and pork. Sear to golden on both sides. Monitor each meat closely as the sausage will be done first, after 2 to 3 minutes. The other pieces of meat will be done soon after—the smaller cuts will cook faster than the larger ones. This is a rustic dish with many types of meat that will cook at different rates. Remove the meat as it is done and set aside.

5 | Add the shallots, carrots, and celery to the same pot. Cook over medium-high heat, stirring occasionally, until soft and golden, about 4 minutes. Add the white pepper, allspice, chicken stock, and pork bone and bring to a boil. Turn down the heat to a light simmer and cook for another 15 minutes. Remove from the heat. Remove the pork bone and reserve. Allow the mixture to cool until you are comfortable transferring it to a blender. Puree the mixture to a smooth consistency and then pour it back into the same pot. Add the pork bone again, along with the cannellini, thyme, herbes de Provence, and 1 teaspoon salt. Bring to a boil, turn down the heat to a simmer, and cook for 10 minutes. Remove and discard the bone. Add all the meat back to the pot, cover the pot tightly, and place the pot on the center rack of the oven. Bake for 10 minutes.

6 | Remove the pot from the oven and stir in the tomatoes.

7 | Turn the oven to broil.

8 | While the oven heats, make the bread crumb topping. In a food processor, add the bread cubes, parsley, and olive oil. Pulse-chop to a coarse bread crumb consistency. You'll get a nice green bread crumb from the parsley chopping into the bread.

9 | Scatter the bread crumbs evenly over the top of the cassoulet. Place the pot in the oven under the broiler. Stand by and watch closely as it takes only a couple of minutes for the bread crumbs to turn golden brown. Remove the pot from the oven and set in the center of the table (on hot pads). Let everyone serve themselves right from the pot.

STRIP STEAK WITH "SECRET" GREEN SAUCE

Normally I steer clear of touristy restaurants in Paris, but Le Relais de l'Entrecôte is irresistible because of its superb secret green sauce. This intoxicating condiment is a rich blend of green flavors so clean and herbaceous you'll want to drink it. Unable to pry the recipe out of the intimidating French waiters, I re-created the recipe on my own. You'll feel like a mad scientist mixing together all the ingredients in this recipe, but trust me, the outcome is well worth it. You can serve this steak with potatoes or the classic *pomme frites* (French fries). Try to resist doing shots of the sauce.

SERVES 8

- 1 tablespoon olive oil
- 1 tablespoon finely chopped garlic
- 1 cup shallots, roughly chopped
- 1½ cups chicken stock
- 1 teaspoon freshly ground black pepper, plus more for seasoning
- 1½ tablespoons Dijon mustard
- ½ cup packed fresh tarragon
- 1½ cups packed fresh flat-leaf parsley
- 1½ tablespoons red wine vinegar
- 1 teaspoon anchovy paste
- 1 teaspoon Worcestershire sauce
- 1 tablespoon unsalted butter
- 1 teaspoon kosher salt, plus more for seasoning
- One 10-ounce hanger steak, New York strip steak, or steak of your choice

1 | First, prepare the sauce. In a medium pot over medium heat, add the olive oil. Add the garlic and shallots and cook until soft and slightly golden. Add the chicken stock. Simmer for 3 minutes and remove from the heat.

2 | In a blender, add the pepper, mustard, tarragon, parsley, vinegar, anchovy paste, Worcestershire, butter, and salt. Carefully pour the chicken stock mixture into the blender and puree until completely smooth. Pour the puree back into the pot and set aside.

3 | Season the steak with an even coat of salt and pepper. Sauté, grill, or broil to medium-rare or desired doneness, about 3 minutes per side. Allow the steak to rest for at least 15 minutes. Cut the steak into 8 slices and lay them on a platter. Pour the green sauce over the steak slices and serve immediately.

BEEF BOURGUIGNON

Good wine reduced down and falling-apart-tender meat made ultrasavory with bacon or pancetta characterize this decadent and hearty one-pot meal, which also has a *Global Kitchen* twist: A very Italian Parmesan rind adds depth of flavor and texture to this signature French recipe.

SERVES 4

3	ounces pancetta or bacon, finely chopped
1	tablespoon olive oil
1½	pounds top sirloin, cut into 1-inch cubes
	Kosher salt and freshly ground black pepper
¾	cup all-purpose flour
10	button mushrooms, stems removed, cut in half
¼	cup roughly chopped shallots
½	cup roughly chopped carrots

½	cup roughly chopped celery
1	tablespoon finely chopped garlic
⅛	cup brandy
1½	cups dry red wine
3	cups beef stock
¼	teaspoon chile flakes
1	bay leaf, ground
2	teaspoons fresh thyme, finely chopped
10	pearl onions, peeled
1	ounce Parmesan cheese rind
3	tablespoons roughly chopped fresh flat-leaf parsley

1 | Place a thick-bottomed ovenproof pot over medium-high heat. Once the pot is hot, add the bacon and cook until golden, about 2 minutes. Pour off the excess fat and discard. Set the bacon aside.

2 | Add 1½ teaspoons of the olive oil to the same pot. Pat the sirloin dry with a paper towel and season well with salt and pepper. Dust the meat with the flour, shaking off any excess right before placing the meat in the pot. You want an even, thin coating all over the meat. Add half the meat to the pot (to avoid overcrowding and steaming instead of searing it). Brown the meat all over, about 15 minutes, and remove from the heat. Set aside.

3 | Add the remaining 1½ teaspoons olive oil and do the same with the second half of the meat. Remove from the heat and set aside with the first half.

4 | Preheat the oven to 275°F.

continued

5 | To the same pot over medium-high heat, add the mushrooms, shallots, carrots, celery, and garlic. Cook until deep golden and soft, about 10 minutes. Manage the heat. You want to build a golden crust in the pan, but do not let it burn. Pour in the brandy and stir. It will be absorbed almost immediately. Cook for 30 seconds. Turn the heat to high and add the red wine. Simmer until the wine is almost fully absorbed. The mixture will be wet but not too liquidy. Add the beef stock, chile flakes, bay leaf, and thyme and boil for about 5 minutes to reduce the stock by one-third. Add the pearl onions, Parmesan rind, and all the meat, and stir. Cover the pot and bake in the oven for 3 hours, or until the meat is super fork-tender.

6 | Place on plates and garnish with the parsley. Enjoy.

FLAVOR SECRETS

When simmered in soups or sauces, Parmesan rind infuses everything with a subtle, rich, slightly nutty flavor. If you buy a chunk of Parmesan, save the rind and keep it in your refrigerator for future use. This is an economical and delicious way to make the most out of Parmesan.

SMOKED AND SAVORY SPAIN

...

Spain is located at the center of a culinary and geographic crossroads. It is a giant peninsula that is surrounded by the Atlantic Ocean and the Mediterranean Sea and bordered by two countries. Its eastern borders are unmistakably European, and from its southernmost point you can practically touch North Africa. Long before King Ferdinand sent Christopher Columbus to establish a sea route to India (for spices, of course), people were crossing Spain's borders and food has been its lingua franca. No wonder its cuisine is a mélange of Mediterranean, Middle Eastern, and European flavor profiles.

My travels in Spain are always centered around food. I begin an average day with a big wedge of aged Manchego whacked off a giant cheese wheel. From there, it's all about tasty tapas (finger foods with attitude): fleshy, sea-infused sardines and grilled octopuses, smoked chorizo and *jamón serrano* (Spain's version of prosciutto, only richer, meatier, saltier, *and* sweeter), golden saffron paellas, and fantastically fresh, tomato-packed gazpachos. And many dishes infused with the fire-red radiance of smoked paprika. Spain's flavor profile is roasted, sweet, savory, and smoky. In these few pages I bring you some of my favorite dishes from a land whose residents sit down for dinner long after most Anglo-Saxons have turned off their bedside lamps.

CHILES

FLAT-LEAF PARSLEY

GARLIC

SAFFRON

SMOKED PAPRIKA

THYME

CHILES See page 5.

FLAT-LEAF PARSLEY (also known as Italian parsley) is far more than a garnish; its deep green leaves pack more flavor than the curly parsley used to decorate finished appetizers and entrées. This supernova of freshness is used to enhance everything from meat, fish, eggs, and veggie dishes to stews, soups, and sauces.

GARLIC is a fundamental element of so many dishes and has a folkloric past (vampires beware!). Called the "stinking rose," garlic's nutty, onionlike flavor attributes vary depending on how you cook the garlic, but the garlic flavor is as basic and vital as salt. And like salt, it's important to use just the right amount of this potent ingredient to bring the flavors together without overpowering the other elements of a dish.

SAFFRON See page 29.

SMOKED PAPRIKA is a mighty but misunderstood spice. Long appreciated as a garnish for deviled eggs, smoked paprika actually makes the best barbecue—chile and heat all in one. Today, smoked paprika is essentially a powder of dried red chiles, but back in the day, Spaniards created this spice by smoking chiles over wood. Anything you cook with smoked paprika smells and tastes as if you pulled it out of a brick oven. It comes sweet or hot, so pick your pleasure, and is ideal for use in eggs and rice dishes—or anytime you want to add a smoky, subtle heat.

THYME See page 29.

SPANISH FLAVOR FAMILY

PAN Y TOMATE TAPAS

You can't walk into a Spanish bar without finding a variation of this classic tapa. The porous bread literally soaks up the intense savory flavors of garlic and sun-ripened tomatoes. The addition of Manchego is my twist and not typical in Spain. This awesome snack or party food is ultraflexible: Add different cheeses or thin slices of leftover meat, olives, or vegetables you might have and customize your tapas. You can also top these tapas with a bit of prosciutto or *jamón serrano* for even more flavor. Anytime I have a really ripe tomato sitting on the counter staring at me (and never store tomatoes in the fridge; refrigeration makes them spongy), I make *pan y tomate*.

SERVES 4

Loaf of rustic bread

3 garlic cloves

2 ripe tomatoes

2 tablespoons extra virgin olive oil

½ cup shredded Manchego cheese

⅓ cup roughly chopped fresh flat-leaf parsley

1 | Cut the bread into 8 slices ½ inch thick and 5 inches long—or similar, depending on the size of your loaf. Grill the bread in a panini press or toast in a toaster. Remove to a large plate.

2 | Rub each slice with garlic. Discard the leftover garlic.

3 | Cut the tomatoes in large wedges and rub them across the top of the bread. Drizzle the bread with the olive oil. Garnish with the Manchego and parsley. Serve on a platter.

FLAVOR SECRETS

The absolute key to this dish is very ripe, sweet tomatoes. You want their juices to explode when you rub the tomatoes across the hot, crispy bread. If you can't find ripe tomatoes, you can use canned plum tomatoes, but be careful not to soak the bread too much.

COD TAPAS WITH RED BELL PEPPER AND ALMOND PUREE

I had a variation of this tapas in a bar in San Sebastián: tender morsels of salt cod rehydrated to perfection and topped with slivers of fried chiles and onions, olives and anchovies. The red bell pepper and almond puree, my personal spin, ups the ante a bit. I use regular cod to save the time of rehydrating salt cod. This dish is a great addition to a tapas spread or accompaniment to a *Tortilla Español* (see page 108). These are great served at room temperature. This is enough for 8 people to have a couple tapas. Adjust based on how many other tapas or appetizers you are serving.

SERVES 4 TO 8

½	tablespoon olive oil, plus more to taste		½	teaspoon dried thyme
½	cup thinly sliced red bell pepper		½	cup chicken stock
¼	cup skinless slivered almonds		1	pound thick cod or whitefish
½	teaspoon roughly chopped garlic		¼	cup water
½	teaspoon kosher salt, plus more for seasoning		16	small baguette rounds
			1	cup canola oil
½	teaspoon smoked paprika		½	pasilla chile or other green chile of your choice, thinly sliced
			½	yellow bell pepper, thinly sliced

1 | In a medium pot over medium heat, add the olive oil. Once the oil is hot, add the red bell pepper and almonds. Stir and cook until golden, about 2 minutes. Add the garlic, salt, paprika, and thyme. Stir just to bring out the aroma of the garlic. Add the chicken stock. Bring to a boil, then lower the heat to just under a simmer and cook for 5 minutes. Transfer the mixture to a blender and puree until smooth. Set aside.

2 | In a medium nonstick skillet over medium heat, add a touch of olive oil. Once the oil is hot, add the cod. Sprinkle with a touch of salt. Add the water to the pan, cover, and cook the cod until done. (When you can push a spoon against the top of the cod and it separates, it is done.) Make sure to keep the heat below a boil. You want to gently steam the cod so it stays tender.

3 | Toast the baguette rounds to golden in a panini press, toaster, or broiler. Lay on a platter.

continued

4 | In a small pot, add the canola oil and heat to 350°F on a frying thermometer, or until a chile dropped into the oil sizzles. Add the sliced pasilla and the yellow bell pepper to the hot oil in two separate batches. Fry for about 3 minutes, until golden. Remove with a slotted spoon and drain on paper towels. Sprinkle with a touch of salt.

5 | To assemble the tapas, spread a small spoonful of the red pepper puree on each baguette round. Break the cod apart and place on the puree. Top the cod with the fried chile and yellow bell pepper. Serve immediately.

FLAVOR SECRETS

I like the heat of the pasilla chile, but you can use a green Anaheim or regular green bell pepper for a milder heat. There is a huge array of chiles that come in many flavors and degrees of heat. The capsaicin in them produces endorphins, which is why spicy food is known to improve a sense of well-being as well as provide a delicious kick to food.

SPANISH STUFFING WITH CHORIZO AND TOASTED ALMONDS

This is stuffing with a Spanish attitude. The flavor-packed oils of pancetta, almonds, and chorizo roast together and melt into their own sauce. Caraway seeds add a floral, earthy perfume. The almonds give it crunch. And the smoked paprika lights up the dish with its brick-red hue and fire-roasted flavor. Leftover stuffing can be sautéed and enjoyed with an egg or a side salad for a meal that is both gorgeous and delicious.

SERVES 8

1 sourdough baguette	½ cup skinless slivered almonds
2 large egg yolks	⅓ cup chorizo sausage (raw or cured and chopped)
1 teaspoon smoked paprika	
½ teaspoon kosher salt	1 teaspoon caraway seeds
⅓ cup roughly chopped pancetta or bacon	2 tablespoons unsalted butter
	2½ cups chicken stock

1 | Cut or tear the baguette into 1-inch cubes.

2 | If you're cooking the stuffing right away, preheat the oven to 400°F.

3 | In a large bowl, combine the egg yolks, paprika, and salt. Set aside.

4 | In a large skillet over medium heat, cook the pancetta until it begins to brown. Add the almonds and chorizo. Stir occasionally and continue cooking until all is evenly golden, about 2 minutes. Add the caraway seeds and cook for 1 more minute to toast the seeds. Turn off the heat and allow to cool briefly. Stir into the egg mixture.

5 | In the same pan over medium heat, melt the butter and add the bread cubes. Stir the bread cubes until they're evenly coated and cook until slightly golden. Remove the bread from the pan and add to the egg mixture. Transfer the entire mixture to a broiler-proof baking dish large enough so that the stuffing fits in one even layer.

6 | If you are making this ahead of time, cover the mixture and refrigerate it until you are ready to cook. Then follow the procedure below.

7 | Pour the chicken stock over the mixture. Cover the baking dish with aluminum foil and bake for 30 minutes, or until all of the liquid is absorbed. Turn the oven to broil and take the foil off the dish. Broil until the top is golden brown. Serve.

CRUSTLESS SWEET ONION AND POTATO SPANISH TART (TORTILLA ESPAÑOL)

Here's a staple on almost every Spanish tapas bar—and it's all about simplicity. Creamy, light sautéed potatoes soaked with a full-flavored olive oil and onions come together in a sweet tart. *Tortilla Español* is delicious as a snack or as a simple main course, served with salad and a glass of white wine.

SERVES 6

4 russet potatoes	2 teaspoons kosher salt, plus more for seasoning
¾ cup extra virgin olive oil	
3 cups thinly sliced Vidalia or yellow onions	1 cup sliced Roma tomatoes or tomatoes of your choice
4 large eggs	½ cup fresh flat-leaf parsley, trimmed of large stems
1 teaspoon smoked paprika	

1 | Peel the potatoes and cut into ⅓-inch-thick slices. If the peeled potatoes will sit for more than a few minutes, keep them in water to prevent browning. Make sure to dry them well before cooking.

2 | In a large nonstick skillet over medium heat, add ¼ cup of the olive oil. Once the oil is hot, add as many potatoes as will fit in one layer. Stir the potatoes well to evenly coat them with oil. (Manage the heat, manage the spud: You want the heat high enough to cook the potatoes, but low enough so they don't get brown or crispy. The potatoes should finish very lightly golden and soft. Move the potatoes around, adjusting for hot spots in the pan. If you're comfortable managing two pans at a time, the process will go faster.)

3 | Cook until barely golden on one side and flip to the other side. Cook until fork-tender. Pour the potatoes and oil into a strainer set over a plate. Save the oil that strains off. Once the potatoes are drained, transfer them to a bowl. Repeat until all the potatoes are cooked. Use the remaining ½ cup olive oil as well as the olive oil that gathers under the strainer for each of the next batches of potatoes.

4 | Once all the potatoes are cooked and drained, return the reserved oil to the same pan and add the onions. Cook until soft and slightly golden, about 5 minutes. Drain off the oil and add the onions to the bowl of potatoes.

5 | In a large bowl, whisk together the eggs, paprika, and salt. Add the potatoes and onions and mix well. Be careful not to break up the potatoes too much.

6 | Add the mixture back into the same nonstick skillet and set over medium heat. Press the mixture down into the pan with a spatula; press down firmly enough so that the mixture forms the shape of the pan. Cook until the bottom is golden, about 6 minutes. Smell close to the pan to make sure it is not burning. Remove from the heat and place a large plate over the pan. Carefully flip the pan over so that the potato goes onto the plate. Place the pan back over the heat and slide the potato mixture back into the pan. Now the golden side is up and you are browning the other side. Cook until the bottom is golden and the mixture is set, about 6 minutes. Remove from the heat. Use the plate to flip the potatoes over once more, but this time, leave the potatoes on the plate.

7 | Salt the tomato slices and use them to garnish the potatoes. Garnish with the parsley. Slice the *Tortilla Español* into small wedges and serve immediately.

ROASTED RED PEPPER SOUP WITH SHERRY AND TOASTED MARCONA ALMONDS

Sherry and almonds are a classic wine and food pairing. By reducing the sherry down with the toasted almonds, the flavor in this soup becomes intriguingly complex. The sherry adds a unique woody, aged flavor that balances brilliantly with the almonds, while the paprika accentuates the bell pepper flavor, creating a velvety pureed delight.

SERVES 4

- 1½ tablespoons olive oil
- 1½ cups finely chopped red bell pepper
- 1 cup chopped shallots
- ½ cup skinless slivered Marcona almonds
- 1 cup dry sherry
- 1 cup tomato puree or chopped canned tomatoes
- 2 cups chicken stock
- 1 tablespoon smoked paprika
- 1½ teaspoons kosher salt
- 2 tablespoons roughly chopped fresh flat-leaf parsley

1 | In a medium pot over medium-high heat, add the olive oil. Once the oil is hot, add the red bell pepper, shallots, and almonds. Keep an eye on the heat and stir frequently to get a golden color without burning. Sauté until evenly golden, about 5 minutes.

2 | Add the sherry and simmer until fully absorbed. Add the tomato puree, chicken stock, paprika, and salt. Cover and simmer over low heat for 20 minutes.

3 | Remove the pot from the heat and allow to cool. Transfer the mixture to a blender and puree until smooth, or keep the soup chunky if you like the texture. Strain the pureed soup if you want it silky smooth.

4 | Ladle the soup into bowls and garnish with the parsley.

OVEN-DRIED TOMATO GAZPACHO WITH PAPRIKA-TOASTED BREAD CUBES AND SAFFRON SOUR CREAM TOPPING

Cold and *soup* are not two words you'd normally put together, unless you're talking about classic Spanish gazpacho. Gazpacho brings the freshest vegetables together in a refreshing soup to cool you down on a hot day. The smoked paprika in the bread cubes accentuates the bell peppers and tops off the sour cream with color and depth of flavor.

SERVES 4

GAZPACHO

- 1 tablespoon extra virgin olive oil
- ½ cup roughly chopped red onion
- ½ cup roughly chopped celery
- 1 tablespoon roughly chopped garlic
- 1 teaspoon smoked paprika
- ¼ cup freshly roasted red bell pepper (canned or jarred optional)
- 2 cups canned plum tomatoes
- 2 cups water
- ¼ cup roasted yellow bell pepper, roughly chopped
- ¼ cup roasted green Anaheim chiles, roughly chopped
- ½ cup oven-dried tomatoes, cut into thirds (see page 112)
- ½ cup peeled and roughly chopped cucumber
- 1 teaspoon kosher salt

BREAD CUBES

- 2 cups cubed rustic bread (1-inch cubes)
- ½ teaspoon smoked paprika
  Pinch of kosher salt
- 1 teaspoon finely chopped garlic
- 2 tablespoons olive oil

SAFFRON SOUR CREAM

- ¼ cup sour cream
- 1 teaspoon saffron water (see Flavor Secrets, page 33)
  Pinch of kosher salt

1 | First, prepare the gazpacho. In a medium pot over medium heat, add the olive oil. Once the oil is hot, add the red onion, celery, and garlic. Cook until slightly golden and soft, about 3 minutes. Add the paprika and stir briefly to toast the spice. Add the roasted red bell pepper, plum tomatoes, and water and bring to a boil. Turn down the heat to low, cover the pot, and cook for 15 minutes. Allow to cool slightly. Transfer to a food processor and puree until slightly chunky.

continued

2 | Pour the puree into a large bowl. Once the puree is cool, stir in the yellow bell pepper, Anaheim chile, oven-dried tomatoes, cucumber, and salt. Refrigerate until very cold.

3 | Preheat the oven to 400°F.

4 | To prepare the croutons, in a bowl, toss the bread cubes with the smoked paprika, salt, garlic, and olive oil. Spread on a sheet pan and toast until golden and crispy, about 2 minutes per side. Set aside to cool.

5 | Next, prepare the saffron sour cream. Pour the sour cream into a small bowl. Stir in the saffron water and salt. Refrigerate for 30 minutes.

6 | Ladle the soup into bowls. Ten minutes before serving, put 3 croutons in each bowl of soup so they start to absorb the soup and soften. They will be crispy and chewy on top and soft on the bottom. Place spoonfuls of the sour cream on top.

Oven-Dried Tomatoes

Preheat the oven to 275°F. Rub 1 tablespoon of olive oil onto a sheet pan. Slice 6 Roma tomatoes (or tomatoes of your choice) into ⅓-inch-thick slices and lay on pan. Drizzle with 2 tablespoons of olive oil and place in oven. Cook until slices have shrunk to ⅓ of their original thickness (about 4 hours). Allow to cool to room temperature. Store covered in the refrigerator for up to 5 days.

SPANISH GRILLED CHEESE SANDWICH WITH SMOKED PAPRIKA SALSA

In this *Global Kitchen* version of an American favorite, grilled cheese is taken to a new level. Smoked paprika adds a burst of fire-roasted chile flavor to the rich, creamy cheeses. Whole-leaf parsley adds a fresh grassy bite, and sherry vinegar and lemon juice impart a bright, cleansing acidity.

SERVES 4

½ cup finely chopped shallots

1 cup whole parsley leaves

2 tablespoons sherry vinegar

1 tablespoon fresh lemon juice

½ teaspoon kosher salt

1½ teaspoons smoked paprika

5 ounces Manchego cheese

5 ounces fontina cheese

2 ounces white cheddar cheese

8 slices white bread

2 tablespoons unsalted butter, at room temperature

⅓ cup roughly chopped fresh flat-leaf parsley (optional)

1 | To make the salsa, in a medium bowl, mix together the shallots, parsley leaves, sherry vinegar, lemon juice, salt, and paprika. Mix well and let sit for at least 20 minutes before serving.

2 | Grate the Manchego, fontina, and white cheddar cheeses into a bowl and mix together.

3 | Lay 4 bread slices out and top each with about 1½ ounces (by weight) of the grated cheese. Spread 1 tablespoon of the salsa evenly across the cheese. (You can also skip the salsa and put just the smoked paprika and whole parsley leaves directly onto the cheese.) Top with the remaining 4 slices of bread and push down slightly.

4 | Spread both sides of each sandwich with the butter. Griddle until golden on both sides and the cheeses are melted, about 2 minutes per side. Serve immediately, garnished with the chopped parsley, if desired.

SAFFRON AND SMOKED PAPRIKA—SPICED SEAFOOD PAELLA

Nothing's more Spanish than paella. Spaniards are passionate about the different ways of making this special short-grain rice and seafood dish. Cooked in a flavorful broth with an endless variety of seafood, meat, or both, this hearty dish is almost like a Spanish version of risotto. You don't have to stir it though, so you end up with separate, whole grains of flavorful rice. Here, you want your garlic to get to a deep, dark brown color. That strong toasted flavor makes this dish a surefire crowd-pleaser, which you can serve as a side dish or as a main course.

SERVES 6

BROTH

- 3 cups chicken stock
- ½ cup tomato puree
- ½ teaspoon kosher salt
- 1 teaspoon saffron water (see Flavor Secrets, page 33)

SEAFOOD

- 5 ounces calamari, cleaned well (tubes and tentacles)
- 5 ounces sea scallops or any whitefish of your choice
- 4 ounces jumbo shrimp
- 1 pound clams
- 1 tablespoon olive oil

Kosher salt and freshly ground black pepper

- ½ cup dry white wine

RICE

- 4 ounces chorizo sausage (cured, not raw)
- 2 tablespoons olive oil
- 2 garlic cloves, thinly sliced
- ¼ cup finely chopped shallots
- ¼ cup finely chopped red bell pepper
- 1 cup cut green beans (1-inch pieces)
- ¾ cup Spanish rice (labeled "Spanish" or "paella" rice; arborio is OK as well)
- 2 teaspoons smoked paprika

1 | First, prepare the broth. In a medium pot over medium heat, heat the chicken stock, tomato puree, salt, and saffron water. Keep hot but do not boil.

2 | While the broth is heating, prepare the seafood. Cut the tubes of calamari into 1-inch rounds. Cut the tentacles in half. Rinse the scallops well and pat dry with a paper towel. Remove and discard the rubbery lip from the side of each scallop. Peel and devein the shrimp (if they're not already cleaned); it's OK to leave the tails on. Discard any open clams, then rinse the clams under cold water and set aside to drain.

3 | In a large skillet over medium-high heat, add the olive oil. Pat the calamari, scallops, and shrimp dry with a paper towel and season with salt and pepper. Place in the skillet so that there is space between the ingredients, allowing them to sear instead of steam. Once they are deep golden on both sides, remove from the skillet and reserve on a plate. It is OK that the seafood is slightly undercooked at this point. Turn down the heat to avoid burning the bottom of the skillet. Add the clams and wine and cover the skillet. Once the clams start to open, remove the lid and let the wine reduce while the clams finish opening. Transfer the clams and juices to a bowl and reserve. Discard any that do not open.

4 | Preheat the oven to 500°F.

5 | Finally, prepare the rice. Cut the chorizo into ¼-inch angular slices, then cut those in half to make strips. This way they disperse nicely and are easy to eat.

6 | In a wide, shallow, ovenproof, thick-bottomed skillet (or a paella pan if you have one) over medium heat, add the olive oil and garlic and allow the garlic to get dark brown. Add the chorizo, shallots, red bell pepper, and green beans. Stir occasionally and cook until golden, about 5 minutes.

7 | Stir in the rice and paprika and cook for 1 minute. Add half of the tomato broth and stir once just to combine. Bring to a boil and let simmer for 3 minutes. Add the remainder of the broth and bring to a boil.

8 | Carefully transfer the skillet to the center rack of the oven. Cook, uncovered, for about 10 minutes, until the liquid is absorbed and the rice is al dente (tender and moist but with a touch of body). Remove the skillet from the oven and spoon the calamari, scallops, and shrimp on top. Place the clams on top of that and pour the juices over. Return the skillet to the oven for 2 minutes. This will allow the seafood to finish cooking and get hot. The juices will soak into the paella and you will have perfectly cooked rice and perfectly cooked seafood.

9 | Place the hot skillet on hot pads on the table. Keep an oven mitt or towel over the handle so no-body gets burned. Serve the paella right out of the pan onto plates. Enjoy!

SQUID INK SPAGHETTI WITH SHRIMP AND CHORIZO

Consider this a Spanish version of surf and turf, with shrimp and chorizo. The contrast of the black pasta with the seared pink shrimp and red chorizo is a visual and gastronomic delight. If you can't find black squid ink pasta, feel free to substitute plain spaghetti or pasta of your choice instead.

SERVES 4

20 jumbo shrimp, with their shells	Freshly ground black pepper
3 tablespoons olive oil	1 pound squid ink spaghetti
⅓ cup shredded carrots	1 teaspoon finely chopped garlic
¼ cup finely chopped shallots	¼ cup chopped chorizo (ideally raw but cured is OK)
½ teaspoon kosher salt, plus more for seasoning	1 tablespoon unsalted butter
½ cup dry white wine	¼ cup fresh flat-leaf parsley, roughly chopped
1 cup Pomi puree or canned chopped tomatoes	

1 | Peel and devein the shrimp. Reserve the shells.

2 | In a large sauté pan over medium-high heat, add 2 tablespoons of the olive oil. Add the shrimp shells, carrots, shallots, and salt. Cook until deep golden, about 5 minutes.

3 | Add the white wine and simmer over high heat until the wine is reduced by half. Add the tomato puree and simmer uncovered for 10 minutes. Remove from the heat and set aside to cool.

4 | Transfer the mixture to a blender and puree until smooth. Strain through a fine-mesh strainer into a bowl and reserve the liquid. Make sure to press on the solids in the strainer to get all the tasty juices out. Discard the solids. (The sauce can be made 1 day ahead.)

5 | To prepare the spaghetti, bring a large pot of water to a boil. Add enough salt to taste it (around ¼ cup). This will bring out the flavor of the pasta.

6 | In a large sauté pan over medium-high heat, add the remaining 1 tablespoon olive oil. Season the shrimp with salt and pepper and add to the pan. Make sure to leave at least 2 inches between the shrimp so they don't overcrowd. (This assures that the shrimp sear instead of boil or steam from too much moisture.) You might need to cook them in two separate batches. Pull the shrimp out when they're opaque. The residual heat will finish cooking the interior.

7 | Drop the spaghetti into the boiling water and cook according to the package instructions until al dente.

8 | While the spaghetti is cooking, return the shrimp to the sauté pan and cook until golden on both sides. Remove from the pan and reserve. To the same pan add the garlic and chorizo. Cook for about 2 minutes, until the chorizo is golden and releases its beautiful red oils. Add the reserved wine-tomato puree and simmer for a few minutes to reduce, thus thickening the sauce slightly and concentrating the flavor.

9 | Once it is al dente, pull the pasta straight out of the cooking water and drop it directly into the sauce. Add a little of the pasta cooking water with the pasta for more flavor. Simmer the pasta in the sauce for 1 minute. Turn off the heat and toss in the shrimp and butter; stir until the butter is evenly melted. Serve the pasta topped with the parsley.

FLAVOR SECRETS

Shrimp shells add a ton of fresh shellfish flavor to sauces—and in a fraction of the time it takes to make a meat or chicken stock. In this recipe, you not only make a quick seafood stock, you get even more flavor by pureeing the shells and liquid together, then straining the shells. Imagine making tea, then squeezing the tea bag, for example.

INDIVIDUAL SMOKED PAPRIKA LASAGNAS

This global kitchen recipe and family favorite is transformed with Spanish flavors and captures all the richness and texture of a lasagna in a fraction of the time. Chorizo, Manchego, parsley, and, most important, the warm, piercing flavor of smoked paprika combine for a dish that is beautiful and appetizing from the first bite.

SERVES 4

2 tablespoons olive oil	1 tablespoon plus 2 teaspoons smoked paprika
4 ounces raw chorizo	½ cup panko bread crumbs
1 pound ground beef	2 tablespoons heavy cream
2 garlic cloves, roughly chopped	1 tablespoon kosher salt
1 cup roughly chopped onions	8 precooked lasagna sheets
½ cup shredded carrots	1 cup fresh flat-leaf parsley, roughly chopped
½ cup roughly chopped celery	
1 cup red wine	1 cup grated Manchego cheese
One 28-ounce can whole plum tomatoes, pureed	2 tablespoons extra virgin olive oil

1 | In a shallow wide pot over medium-high heat, add the olive oil. Once the oil is hot, add the chorizo and ground beef. Using a spatula, break up the meat as small as you can so it browns. Once it starts to brown, add the garlic, onions, carrots, and celery. Sauté until the mixture is dark brown and well roasted. Constantly scrape the bottom and sides of the pan to incorporate all the flavorful meats and juices into the sauce.

2 | Add the red wine and continue scraping the bottom of the pan. Simmer for 1 minute, or until the wine is reduced by half. Add the tomatoes, 1 tablespoon of the smoked paprika, the panko, cream, and salt. Cover, turn down the heat to very low, and cook for 15 minutes.

3 | Meanwhile, bring a large pot of salted water to a boil. Boil the lasagna sheets according to the package instructions. Drain and set aside. If they are going to sit longer than 5 minutes, toss the sheets in a touch of olive oil so they don't stick together.

4 | On four plates, assemble the ingredients equally in the following order: Lay 1 sheet of pasta on each plate. Spoon the meat mixture over the pasta sheet and spread it out evenly. Sprinkle on some of the parsley and Manchego. Lay another sheet of pasta on top. Sprinkle more parsley and Manchego on top. Dust each plate with ½ teaspoon of the remaining smoked paprika. Drizzle with the extra virgin olive oil. Serve immediately.

SWEET AND SOUR ASIA

...

O n a recent trip to Hong Kong and Shanghai, my palate was ablaze cooking and eating with Asian epicures of all sorts. They introduced me to street lunches of *mala tang* (soup made to order in huge woks) and soup-filled buns in eight-hundred-seat restaurants, wet and dry markets, divine dim sum, dumplings, outrageous noodle dishes, fish maw, and salt-preserved thousand-year-old eggs.

The sweet and sour flavor contrasts that typify Asian cuisine are marked by exquisite simplicity, sensational textures, and an incredible range of heat. Asian jar sauces like hoisin, ponzu, and oyster, and the red devil mega-heat of Sriracha, boost the flavors of staples like rice, noodles, and seafood and are easily reinterpreted across culinary borders. This chapter is a tiny taste of them all.

FENNEL SEEDS

FIVE-SPICE POWDER

GINGER

HOISIN SAUCE

OYSTER SAUCE

PONZU

SOY SAUCE

SRIRACHA SAUCE

FENNEL SEEDS, a world traveler that features prominently in various regional cuisines (see page 51), are an unmistakable part of the Asian flavor family.

FIVE-SPICE POWDER, true to its name, is a blend of five quintessential Asian flavors: the cleansing licorice tastes of fennel seed and star anise, the sweetness of cinnamon and cloves, and the sharp floral finish of Szechuan peppercorns. Like a tasty barbecue rub, five-spice instantly and exotically kicks up the flavor of meats, while also creating a sweet, caramelized crust on the outside.

GINGER is as important to Asian cooking as garlic is to Italian cooking. Ginger packs both a piercing sweetness and a long, slow spiciness like a cross between a Vidalia onion and black pepper. As tasty raw (a popular garnish for sushi) as it is simmered in a rich broth, ginger has long been an important part of Chinese medicine and is used worldwide to treat digestive ailments.

HOISIN SAUCE is a mix of fermented soybeans and wheat with a sweet undertone. This Asian barbecue sauce deliciously thickens gravies and stir-fries and perfectly complements staples like *pho* and fish dishes (perhaps that's why it sounds so much like the Chinese word for "seafood").

OYSTER SAUCE, like hoisin, has a barbecue quality, but features an unmistakable savoriness—umami—much like the taste of oysters. *Umami*, Japanese for "delicious taste," is the "fifth taste" (after sweet, salty, bitter, and sour) and activates the taste buds, heightening their sensitivities to food. MSG is the synthetic (and troublesome) form of umami, but natural sources such as anchovy paste, sun-dried tomatoes, and mushrooms are better.

PONZU is a citrus fruit extraction, usually with a splash of soy. Cooking with ponzu is an excellent way to add lots of flavor without weighing down a dish. Essentially an Asian vinaigrette, ponzu makes an excellent dressing for Chinese chicken salads.

SOY SAUCE is the bedrock of Asian cuisine. This condiment made from fermented soybeans has a salty, earthy flavor that's rich with umami. We take this powerhouse sauce for granted—it's on the tables at almost every Chinese and Japanese restaurant—but it is a labor-intensive artisanal product when made traditionally.

SRIRACHA SAUCE is a piercingly hot and tangy red chile sauce found in many Asian dishes, like Grilled Tilapia in Spicy Asian Broth (page 138) and Hot-and-Sour Soup (page 130). This paste of sun-ripened chiles and garlic adds an intense, brighter heat than the relatively smoky tastes of Mexican salsa or chile condiments.

ASIAN FLAVOR FAMILY

SAVORY CRAB PANCAKES WITH SWEET AND SPICY HOISIN SAUCE

Pancakes are not just for breakfast. Prepare a simple batter, then drop chunks of savory crabmeat onto the pancakes. The crabmeat bursts into a true flavor bomb that's sweet, sour, *and* spicy, thanks to the star sauce here: hoisin. The result is simple yet decadent—a delectable appetizer that can easily become a main course because it's impossible to eat just one of them!

MAKES 12 PANCAKES

1¼ cups rice flour

1 teaspoon kosher salt

1 cup coconut milk

½ cup water

4 large eggs

2 tablespoons sesame seeds

1 tablespoon peanut oil

8 ounces crabmeat

4 tablespoons fresh mint, roughly chopped

4 tablespoons fresh cilantro, roughly chopped

¼ cup Sweet and Spicy Hoisin Sauce

1 | In a medium bowl, mix together the rice flour, salt, coconut cream, water, and eggs. Whisk until smooth. Set aside.

2 | In a nonstick skillet over medium heat, add the sesame seeds. Toast until golden, about 2 minutes. Remove from the pan (to stop cooking) to a plate or to a small bowl. Set aside.

3 | In a large nonstick skillet over medium heat, add 1 teaspoon of peanut oil for each batch of pancakes. Once the oil is hot, add ¼-cup scoops of batter to the pan to form pancakes. When the pancakes bubble on top, drop in some of the crabmeat, mint, and cilantro, then flip over. Sprinkling the herbs into the batter creates an even amount of herbs in each pancake and looks great. Cook until golden, about 2 minutes. Place on a serving plate and cover with aluminum foil to keep warm until all the pancakes are finished.

4 | Garnish with the hoisin sauce, some of the remaining mint and cilantro, and a sprinkle of the toasted sesame seeds. Serve immediately.

Sweet and Spicy Hoisin Sauce

In a medium mixing bowl, stir togerther ½ cup of soy sauce, ¾ cup of Hoisin sauce, and 1 teaspoon of finely chopped serrano chiles. (You can remove the seeds for a less spicy sauce.) Serve immediately.

RED CHILE AND COCONUT MILK SEAFOOD RICE

An intriguing, delicious dish. The fish is tender, the coconut milk is creamy but not rich, and the chile paste has a unique fermented chile flavor that melts into the sauce.

SERVES 4

1½	cups Chinese-style short-grain white rice (aka sticky rice)
3¼	cups water
2	tablespoons rice wine vinegar
1	tablespoon sugar
2	teaspoons kosher salt, plus more for seasoning
½	pound black mussels
1	tablespoon sesame oil
½	pound monkfish or whitefish of your choice
¼	cup finely chopped shallots
2	teaspoons finely chopped ginger
2	teaspoons finely chopped garlic
One	14-ounce can coconut milk
½	cup green beans
1	tablespoon gochujang (see Flavor Secrets, page 127) or red chile paste
2	tablespoons fresh lime juice
2	green onions, roughly chopped
¼	cup fresh cilantro, roughly chopped

1 | In a medium pot over medium-high heat, mix together the rice, 2¼ cups of the water, the vinegar, sugar, and 1 teaspoon of the salt. Bring to a boil. Turn down the heat to low, cover, and cook until the water is absorbed and the rice is tender, about 20 minutes. Set aside.

2 | Remove the beards of the mussels. They look like a thin string hanging out of the shell. Pull that string to the end of the mussel and pull against the end of the shell to remove it. Discard any open shells. Rinse off the mussels and set aside to dry.

3 | In a large pot over medium-high heat, add the sesame oil. Season the monkfish with salt and add to the hot oil. Sauté on both sides to golden, about 1½ minutes on each side. You do not want the fish to be cooked all the way through as it will finish cooking later. Remove the fish and set aside on a plate.

4 | To the same pot, add the shallots, ginger, and garlic and cook for 1 minute. Add the mussels and stir. Cook for 30 seconds. Add the coconut milk, green beans, the remaining 1 cup water, and the gochujang. Mix well. Bring to a boil and then turn down the heat to low and cook until the mussels

open (remove and discard any that don't open). Add the precooked monkfish, the lime juice, the remaining 1 teaspoon salt, and half of the green onions and half of the cilantro. Cook for 1 minute and remove from the heat.

5 | Divide the cooked rice among four plates. Top with equal parts seafood and sauce and garnish with the remaining green onions and cilantro.

FLAVOR SECRETS

Gochujang is a fermented soybean/red chile paste from Korea. It has that "magical" umami quality (heightened flavor enhancer). You can find it online or in an Asian specialty food store. Use red chile paste as an alternative.

CHINESE CHOPPED CHICKEN SALAD WITH "WOK"-FRIED SPICY PEANUTS

Chinese chopped chicken salad is a classic on both sides of the Pacific and a bestseller at the Grove in San Francisco. Use a lightly salted peanut with no skin or a blanched white peanut—avoid cocktail-style peanuts with brown skins on them. You can substitute a tablespoon of soy sauce if you don't want the citrus taste of ponzu. Whichever sauce you choose, the combination of crunchy lettuces and flavorful dressing creates a delectable small, tapas-style plate or a nutritious (but not heavy) full meal.

SERVES 2 TO 4

12	ounces skinless, boneless chicken breasts	½	cup peanuts (see headnote)
1	head romaine lettuce, shredded very thin	1	teaspoon sugar
½	head iceberg lettuce, shredded	½	teaspoon chile flakes
1	carrot, shredded	¼	cup rice wine vinegar
1	cup fresh cilantro, roughly chopped	2	tablespoons fresh orange juice
1	teaspoon peanut oil	1	tablespoon ponzu
		1	tablespoon soy sauce
		¼	cup sesame oil

1 | Poach the chicken (see page 39). Allow to cool, then cut into ½-inch cubes.

2 | In a salad bowl, combine the romaine, iceberg lettuce, carrot, and cilantro.

3 | To prepare the "wok"-style peanuts, in a medium skillet over medium-high heat, add the peanut oil, peanuts, sugar, and chile flakes. Stir occasionally until the peanuts have small char marks on them but are not burned, 2 to 3 minutes. Transfer to a plate to cool.

4 | In a small bowl, whisk together the rice wine vinegar, orange juice, ponzu, soy sauce, and sesame oil until well combined. Adjust the seasoning to taste. Toss all the ingredients together with the dressing and serve.

HOT-AND-SOUR SOUP

Sriracha lights a fire in this soup. One sip and your mouth puckers with the familiar bright acidity of rice wine vinegar and the intense heat from the Sriracha (use half the suggested amount for a less spicy dish). The umami of the soy sauce adds a layer of flavor, and the texture has a delectable viscosity. This is Asia's version of Grandma's chicken soup—only better!

SERVES 4

1   tablespoon cornstarch
1   tablespoon cool water
1   tablespoon toasted sesame oil
4   ounces white mushrooms, thinly sliced
4   green onions, thinly sliced
1   teaspoon finely chopped ginger
1   teaspoon finely chopped garlic
½   cup rice wine vinegar

1   teaspoon sugar
1   tablespoon low-sodium soy sauce
½   teaspoon kosher salt
2   teaspoons Sriracha or red chile sauce
1   quart chicken stock
2   large eggs
½   cup firm tofu, cut into ½-inch cubes
½   cup fresh cilantro, roughly chopped

1 | In a small bowl, mix together the cornstarch and water and set aside.

2 | In a large pot over medium-high heat, add the sesame oil. Once the oil is hot, add the mushrooms. Cook for 1 minute, until soft; they will not have much color. Add the green onions, ginger, and garlic. Cook for 2 minutes. Add the rice wine vinegar, sugar, soy sauce, salt, and Sriracha. Cook for 2 minutes to infuse all the flavors.

3 | Add the chicken stock and bring to a boil. While whisking the soup, slowly pour in the cornstarch mixture. Whisk until combined and the soup starts to thicken. Turn off the heat.

4 | In a small bowl, beat the eggs until just mixed. Slowly pour the eggs into the pot, stirring constantly in a circular motion. Continue to stir for 30 seconds. You will see the egg cook into long, thin strands and the soup will take on a creamy look, although it will still have a broth consistency.

5 | Add the tofu to the soup and garnish with the cilantro. Serve immediately.

FIVE-SPICE SHRIMP SLIDERS

The art of great cooking is making people want more. That's the brilliance of these sliders. Like tapas, these small bites make you want to keep grazing. The five-spice-seared shrimp have a sweet, golden, crispy coating. The star anise, with its naturally high sugar content, caramelizes the outside. Everything comes together with mirin, fresh ginger, garlic, shallots, and the spicy, crunchy heat of pickled cabbage.

SERVES 4

- ½ cup rice wine vinegar
- 1 tablespoon Sriracha sauce
- 2½ teaspoons finely chopped ginger
- 1½ teaspoons kosher salt
- 2 tablespoons ketchup
- ½ head napa cabbage, shredded (4 cups)
- 4 medium green onions, roughly chopped
- ½ cup shredded carrots

- ¼ cup roughly chopped cilantro, plus more for garnish (optional)
- 1 pound shrimp, peeled and deveined
- 1 tablespoon five-spice powder
- 2 tablespoons sesame oil
- 1 garlic clove, finely chopped
- ¼ cup finely chopped shallots
- ¼ cup mirin
- ⅓ cup mayonnaise
- 8 slider buns or rolls, or 4 hot dog buns, cut in half

1 | First, prepare the slaw. In a blender, combine the rice wine vinegar, Sriracha, 1 teaspoon of the ginger, 1 teaspoon of the salt, and the ketchup. Puree until smooth. Set aside.

2 | Place the cabbage in a large bowl. Add the vinegar puree, the green onions, carrots, and cilantro and mix well. Pour into a large casserole dish and press down flat. Cover tightly with plastic wrap and let sit at room temperature for 2 hours or in the refrigerator overnight. Stir occasionally to keep the ingredients well mixed so that the cabbage "pickles."

3 | Pat the shrimp dry with a paper towel. In a medium bowl, toss the shrimp with the five-spice powder and the remaining ½ teaspoon salt to coat evenly and thoroughly.

continued

4 | In a large sauté pan over medium-high heat, add the sesame oil. Once the oil is hot, add the shrimp and sauté until golden, about 1 minute on each side. If your pan is not large enough to avoid overcrowding of the shrimp, do this in two separate batches using 1 tablespoon sesame oil for each batch. Moderate the heat so that you do not burn the spice on the bottom of the pan during the second batch. Remove from the pan to a plate.

5 | To the same pan, add the garlic, the remaining 1½ teaspoons ginger, and the shallots. Sauté until golden, about 2 minutes. Add the mirin and cook until absorbed. It will look like a thick sauce. Transfer to a medium bowl and add the mayonnaise. Chop the shrimp into ½-inch pieces and add to the bowl, mixing to evenly coat the shrimp in the sauce.

6 | Place the slider buns on a plate. Scoop out any extra bread from inside the buns. Spoon the shrimp mixture onto the bottom. Add a large spoonful of the cabbage mixture on top of the shrimp. Let it spill over. Close the bun if desired, serve on a plate with a garnish of cilantro or a little more of the slaw.

ASIAN TURKEY BURGERS

Turkey burgers are a great change of pace from a richer beef burger. The leeks are the secret to the moistness of this burger, heightened by the hoisin and soy sauces, which caramelize on the grill. The panko bread crumbs absorb the juices from the leeks, and the burger becomes almost like an amazing meat loaf. This is the juiciest turkey you'll ever have, and when paired with Sweet and Spicy Chinese Long Beans, it showcases all the flavors of savory Asian barbecue.

SERVES 4

3 large leeks	½ teaspoon kosher salt, plus more for seasoning
1½ teaspoons unsalted butter	Freshly ground black pepper
1½ teaspoons olive oil	4 hamburger buns
1½ pounds ground turkey	Sriracha sauce or other condiment of your choice
¾ cup panko bread crumbs	
1½ tablespoons soy sauce	
2 tablespoons hoisin sauce	

1 | Cut off the dark green parts of the leeks and discard. Cut the leeks in half. Pull out the hard yellow cores and discard. Rinse the cut leeks under cold water, pulling back the folds to get the water in between. (Leeks can be very dirty. This is an important step.) Slice the leeks thinly. You should have about 2 cups.

2 | In a medium skillet over medium to medium-low heat, add the butter and olive oil. Once the butter is melted, add the leeks and cook, stirring occasionally, for about 15 minutes, closely monitoring the heat so that the leeks soften but do not brown. Set aside to cool.

3 | Turn on a grill to medium-high. (Or you can use a cast-iron skillet or a griddle pan set over medium-high heat.) In a medium bowl, add the turkey, panko, soy sauce, hoisin sauce, the cooled leeks, and the salt. Use a fork to combine it all thoroughly, but do not overwork the mixture or the burgers will be tough.

4 | Form the mixture into 4 equal-size patties. Push your thumb into the center of each burger so that the burger does not bulge as it cooks. Season with salt and pepper and place on the hot grill. Cook for about 4 minutes on each side, until cooked through but still juicy (peek if you have to). Once you have a nice sear on the burgers, turn down the heat to medium to fully cook the turkey without burning the outside.

5 | Toast the buns on a grill or under a broiler, if you like. Place the open buns on a plate and spread with Sriracha sauce or another condiment. Place the burgers on top. Serve immediately.

Sweet and Spicy Chinese Long Beans

Rinse and dry 4 cups long beans. Cut into 2-inch pieces. In a wok or large skillet over high heat, add 1½ tablespoons peanut oil, ½ teaspoon chile flakes, and 1 whole garlic clove. (Adjust the chile flakes to the desired level of heat.) When the oil has a haze over it—almost smoking—add the long beans to the pan. Toss them constantly with tongs until they're blistered and slightly golden, about 5 minutes. Add ¼ cup of peanuts and toss for 1 more minute. Add 1 teaspoon fennel seed and stir twice to toast but do not let them burn. Add ¼ cup hoisin and ¼ cup soy sauce and turn off the heat. Stir to evenly coat the beans with the hoisin and soy sauce. There should be enough sauce to run on the plate. Using a heatproof rubber spatula to get the sauce out of the pan, lay the beans on small plates. Serve immediately. (Yields four 1-cup servings.)

STAR ANISE—SCENTED *PHO*

I first had *pho* (pronounced "fa") in France in a Vietnamese restaurant. The broth in this recipe is much lighter than the others in this book, but it's full of flavor from fresh cilantro, basil, and star anise, the "secret" ingredient that adds a mild background note of woodsy licorice. The best part of eating *pho* is making it your own. Use chiles to kick up the heat to your desired level of pain!

SERVES 4

2	ounces glass noodles or rice noodles
One	10-ounce pork chop, bone in
2	teaspoons kosher salt, plus more for seasoning
	Freshly ground black pepper
8	medium shrimp, peeled and deveined
1	tablespoon peanut oil
1	yellow onion, thinly sliced
1	tablespoon finely chopped garlic
1	star anise pod

6	cups chicken stock
One	3-inch piece lemongrass, thinly sliced vertically (optional)
1	tablespoon fresh lime juice
½	bunch fresh cilantro, roughly chopped
1	carrot, shredded
16	fresh basil leaves, stacked, rolled, and thinly sliced
1	serrano or jalapeño chile, sliced into thin disks (remove seeds to make less spicy)
1	cup mung bean sprouts
1	lime, cut into 4 wedges

1 | Bring a pot of water big enough to cook the noodles to a boil. Once the water is boiling, drop in the noodles and cook until al dente (slightly firm). Drain and rinse under cold water to stop the cooking. Shake off the excess water and set aside the noodles to drain. This can be done ahead of time, and the noodles kept, covered, in the refrigerator.

2 | Pat the pork dry, cut the meat off the bone, and save the bone. Cut the meat into 1-inch pieces about ⅓ inch thick. Season with salt and pepper.

3 | Pat the shrimp dry with a paper towel and season with salt and pepper.

4 | In a wide pot over medium-high heat, add the peanut oil. Once the oil is hot, add the pork. Sauté on both sides until golden but slightly undercooked. Transfer to a plate and set aside.

5 | To the same pot, add the shrimp. Sauté until golden, flip over, and cook until the shrimp goes from translucent to opaque. Be careful not to overcook. Transfer to the plate with the pork and set aside.

6 | To the same pot, add the onions, garlic, and pork bone. Cook until a light golden color, about 3 minutes. Grind the star anise pod in a coffee grinder into small pebble-size pieces and add to the pot. Add the chicken stock, 2 teaspoons salt, and lemongrass, if using, and bring to a boil. Cover the pot and turn down the heat to low. Cook for at least 30 minutes but ideally for 2 hours. The flavor will improve with the extended time.

7 | Using a fine-mesh strainer set over a clean bowl, strain the broth into the bowl and discard the solids. Return the broth to the pot and let sit for a few minutes. Using a ladle, skim off and discard the fat that rises to the top.

8 | Add the lime juice, pork, shrimp, and noodles to the pot and bring to a boil. Remove from the heat immediately, or the pork and shrimp will get tough.

9 | Line up four soup bowls. Divide the pork and shrimp among the bowls. Using tongs, divide the noodles among the bowls. Ladle the broth over the top. Top each bowl evenly with the cilantro, carrots, basil, chiles, mung bean sprouts, and lime wedges. Serve immediately.

GRILLED TILAPIA IN SPICY ASIAN BROTH

I won the Red Lobster challenge with this recipe—which landed on Red Lobster's menu in eight hundred locations. Tilapia, scallops, and shrimp are dusted with wasabi powder and seared, brilliantly contrasting with sweet mirin and the salty soy. The grilled tilapia falls apart in the broth. Light and packed with tons of flavor—this dish offers the best of Asia's clean flavors.

SERVES 4

4 tablespoons sesame oil

1 cup roughly chopped shrimp with their shells and tails, plus 4 whole peeled and deveined shrimp

1 cup roughly chopped scallops, plus 4 whole scallops

4 shallots, finely chopped

6 garlic cloves, finely chopped

½ cup mirin

¼ cup soy sauce

¼ cup rice wine vinegar

2 cups water

1¼ cups roughly chopped fresh cilantro

Two 6-ounce tilapia or rock cod fillets

Kosher salt and freshly ground black pepper

1 tablespoon wasabi powder

4 teaspoons Sriracha or red chile sauce

½ cup fresh basil, chopped

3 green onions, chopped

½ carrot, chopped

1 | In a large sauté pan over medium-high heat, heat 3 tablespoons of the sesame oil. Add the chopped shrimp, chopped scallops, the shallots, and garlic. Cook until lightly golden, about 4 minutes. Add the mirin, soy sauce, and rice wine vinegar and simmer for about 5 minutes. Add the water and 1 cup of the cilantro and bring to a boil. Turn down the heat and simmer the broth until reduced by one-third, about 20 minutes. Strain the broth into a bowl and discard the solids.

2 | Preheat a grill or grill pan to medium-high.

3 | Season the tilapia with salt and pepper. Grill until the tilapia is tender and flakes easily. Set aside.

4 | Meanwhile, toss the whole shrimp in the wasabi and season with salt and pepper.

5 | In a medium sauté pan, heat the remaining 1 tablespoon sesame oil. Cook the whole shrimp and whole scallops until golden on both sides, about 1½ minutes per side. Set aside.

6 | Place 1 teaspoon Sriracha sauce in the bottom of each of four soup bowls. Ladle about ½ cup of the broth into each bowl. Stir to gently mix the broth and the Sriracha. Place ½ tilapia fillet in the broth, then add 1 shrimp and 1 scallop. Garnish with the remaining ¼ cup cilantro, the basil, green onions, and carrot. Serve immediately.

GARLIC AND BLACK PEPPER SURF AND TURF STIR-FRY

The natural heat in this stir-fry comes from a heavy dose of garlic and black pepper. A touch of orange juice creates a perfect sweet acidity. Delicious rings of calamari pick up the seared flavors of tender chunks of filet mignon served over the quintessential Asian base of sticky rice.

SERVES 4

12	ounces filet mignon or any good-quality beef, cut into 1-inch pieces
1	tablespoon hoisin sauce
1	tablespoon soy sauce
1½	tablespoons finely chopped garlic
1	tablespoon freshly ground black pepper
10	ounces calamari, cleaned well, tentacles cut in half and tubes cut into ¼-inch rings (you can have your fishmonger do this)
2	heads baby bok choy
1½	cups Chinese-style short-grain white rice (aka sticky rice)
2¼	cups water
1	teaspoon kosher salt, plus more for seasoning
1	tablespoon peanut oil
	Pinch of chile flakes
¼	cup fresh orange juice
2	tablespoons roughly chopped fresh cilantro

1 | In a medium bowl, place the filet mignon. Add the hoisin sauce, soy sauce, 1 tablespoon of the garlic, and 1½ teaspoons of the pepper and mix thoroughly. Cover tightly with plastic wrap and refrigerate for 3 to 6 hours.

2 | In a medium bowl, combine the calamari, the remaining 1½ teaspoons garlic, and the remaining 1½ teaspoons pepper. Cover tightly with plastic wrap and refrigerate for 3 to 6 hours.

3 | Wash and dry the bok choy and cut into 1-inch strips. Set aside.

4 | Pull the beef and calamari out of the refrigerator 30 minutes before cooking so that they come to room temperature. This allows the meat to cook evenly and without creating extra liquid.

5 | In a medium pot, combine the rice, water, and salt. Bring to a boil, then immediately turn down the heat to low, cover, and cook until tender, about 20 minutes. Once the rice is tender, remove it from the heat and let sit, uncovered, for 5 minutes to release the heat. Replace the lid and let sit until you are ready to eat.

continued

6 | Wipe any excess marinade off the beef and calamari, then season with salt.

7 | Place a wok or large skillet over high heat. Once the pan is very hot, add 1½ teaspoons of the peanut oil and the chile flakes and heat until a haze comes off the oil. Add the beef (if your pan is not big enough, cook in several batches so that the pan is never overcrowded). Stir the beef to make sure it is not sticking and that it is evenly coated with the oil. Cook until the beef is golden, about 4 minutes. Transfer the meat onto a plate. The beef should be soft to the touch for a medium-rare serving.

8 | Add the remaining 1½ teaspoons peanut oil to the pan. Add the calamari and stir continuously just until the calamari turns white, about 1 minute. Transfer to the plate with the beef.

9 | Add the bok choy to the pan and cook for 1 minute, stirring continuously. The bok choy should just wilt but still have body. Add the orange juice and stir it around to clean the pan and bring the flavors together. Return the beef and calamari to the pan with the bok choy. Turn off the heat and stir together.

10| Spoon the beef, calamari, and sauce equally over the rice. Garnish with the cilantro.

SPICY BEEF PAD THAI

Pad Thai is a spicy play on sweet and sour that's simple to make and easy to reinvent—simply throw almost any veggie or source of protein you'd like into it (a very Asian attribute). Here, the oyster sauce and egg lend a nice creaminess that makes all the noodles stick together. This is a high-heat, quick-cooking process, so it's important to have all of your ingredients lined up by the stove and ready to go.

SERVES 3 TO 4

1	package thin, dry rice noodles
¼	cup oyster sauce
2	tablespoons low-sodium soy sauce
⅓	cup low-sodium chicken stock
1	large egg
1½	tablespoons peanut oil
8	ounces skirt steak, cut into thin 1-inch-long slices (you can substitute chopped scallops or shrimp)
1	small Thai chile or serrano chile, chopped small
¼	cup finely chopped shallots
1	cup finely chopped broccoli
¼	cup finely chopped peanuts
½	cup roughly chopped green onions
1	cup mung bean sprouts

1 | Bring a pot of water big enough to cook the noodles to a boil. Once the water is boiling, drop in the noodles and cook until al dente (slightly firm). Drain and rinse under cold water to stop the cooking. Shake off the excess water and set aside the noodles to drain. Once they are drained, lay them out on a plate to minimize clumping. The noodles will be cold when added to the pot.

2 | In a small bowl, mix together the oyster sauce, soy sauce, chicken stock, and egg. This is your sauce.

3 | In a wok or large sauté pan over high heat, add 1 tablespoon of the peanut oil. Once you see a haze coming off the oil, add the steak, chile, and shallots. Stir frequently until slightly colored, about 30 seconds, and remove to a plate or bowl.

continued

4 | Add the remaining 1½ teaspoons peanut oil to the wok, then add the broccoli. Cook for 30 seconds and remove to the plate with the steak. Add the peanuts and toast briefly. Add the noodles to the wok and mix with the peanuts. Spread the noodles out thin and cook, without stirring, for 20 seconds.

5 | Add the sauce and half of the green onions to the wok and stir. Add the steak and broccoli and ¾ cup of the bean sprouts. Stir and divide evenly among three or four plates. Garnish each plate with some of the remaining bean sprouts and green onions. Serve immediately.

SPICE
NIRVANA
INDIA

...

India is the *El Dorado of spices.* It literally kicked off the spice trade centuries ago when explorers crossed uncharted seas and risked their lives for its cinnamon, cloves, ginger, cardamom, saffron, turmeric, curry, garam masala, and much more. Today, India is still the largest producer and consumer of spices in the world, exporting 180 different spices to more than 150 countries.

Although I've never been to India, cooking with its native spices was a natural progression after cooking with Mexican spices for decades. The techniques of roasting and toasting seeds (in this case in ghee, or clarified butter) to release their precious oils and bring out the depth of their flavors is popular in both cuisines, as is layering flavors and scents.

The ten dishes featured in this chapter are just a small window into the colorful and fragrant universe that is India.

CARDAMOM

CINNAMON

CUMIN

FENUGREEK

GARAM MASALA

MUSTARD SEEDS

TURMERIC

CARDAMOM See page 29.

CINNAMON is one of the oldest and most important spices known to humankind. Harvested from bark, not fruit, cinnamon is in almost every ethnic cuisine's spice blend—whether sweet or savory. For the best profile of its spicy, bitter, *and* sweet flavor and warm, woody back notes, it's worth the extra money to buy higher-grade cinnamon or to buy it whole and grind it yourself. You'll be amazed at the difference in perfume, flavor, and potency.

CUMIN See page 5.

FENUGREEK is a classic Indian spice found in many dishes. Used in many curries, fenugreek has a sweet, musty smell that is recognizably Indian.

GARAM MASALA, an aromatic and piquant spice blend, is the base of many curries and other Indian flavor combinations. Like the Asian five-spice powder, there are five ingredients that make it rock: the sweet baking spices of cinnamon and nutmeg, along with cumin, black pepper, and cardamom. It is usually added to a dish while it's cooking and then stirred in once more prior to serving for added depth of flavor.

MUSTARD SEEDS give Indian food its signature hot, piquant, rustic buzz, and are the base of the yellow mustard Americans and Europeans know and love. The seeds yield the direct heat and essence of mustard in its purest form, plus a textured crunch. Toasting mustard seeds prior to use is critical to eliminate their bitter undertones and bring out their precious oils.

TURMERIC See page 29.

INDIAN FLAVOR FAMILY

SWEET AND SPICY RED CHILE AND CUCUMBER RAITA

Raita is a yogurt-based staple that crosses borders, from the Middle East (*laban*) to Greece (*tzatziki*) to India. This version of raita is spicy and totally different from its mild cousins around the world. This goes excellently with pita bread or flatbread, or as a condiment for dishes like Tandoori-Style Chicken with Basmati Rice and Spicy Tomato Chutney (page 161) and Turmeric Grilled Scallop Pitas (page 157).

MAKES 2½ CUPS RAITA

1 large English cucumber, peeled and diced small (1½ cups)	1 teaspoon finely diced red jalapeño pepper
½ teaspoon cumin seed	2 teaspoons sugar
½ teaspoon coriander seed	½ teaspoon kosher salt
¼ cup fresh cilantro, roughly chopped	1 cup plain yogurt

1 | In a bowl large enough to allow the cucumber to lie in one or two layers, add the cucumber.

2 | In a small, dry pan over medium heat, toast the cumin and coriander just until you smell them. Allow to cool for a few minutes, then grind them finely. Stir into the cucumber.

3 | In a small bowl, add the cilantro, jalapeño, sugar, and salt and stir together. Stir into the cucumber. Allow to sit out at room temperature for 2 hours, stirring occasionally. The salt and sugar will draw out the juice of the cucumber, soften the texture of the spices, and marry all the flavors.

4 | Add the yogurt and stir. Chill in the refrigerator for a few hours, or ideally overnight, to bring out the flavors.

DAL WITH GARAM MASALA

Many variations of dal accompany Indian meals. The garam masala in this recipe is flavorful and spicy but not hot. The dal has a souplike consistency and can be eaten in small portions right out of the bowl as an appetizer, or served as a dip with naan or pita bread.

SERVES 4

1 tablespoon canola oil

1 tablespoon unsalted butter

¾ cup finely chopped yellow onion

2 teaspoons ground turmeric

¾ cup yellow split peas

3 cups chicken stock

2 teaspoons garam masala

1 teaspoon kosher salt

¼ cup finely chopped fresh cilantro

1 | In a medium pot over medium heat, add the canola oil and butter. Once the oil and butter are hot, add the onion and cook until soft and golden, about 3 minutes. Stir in the turmeric and cook for 2 minutes longer, until golden. Add the split peas, chicken stock, and garam masala and bring to a boil. Cover and turn down the heat to low. Cook for 45 minutes, or until the split peas fall apart.

2 | Whisk the split peas until mostly smooth. The texture will still be a little coarse. Stir in the salt. Spoon into small bowls and garnish with the cilantro. Serve immediately.

CURRIED SWEET PEA SOUP WITH BUTTERED WHITE PEPPER BREAD CRUMBS

Sometimes the random food I have in my freezer and refrigerator yields some of my best recipes. Curried sweet pea soup is a good example. Turmeric's yellow color is masked by the green peas, but its earthy mustardlike flavor glows along with the chile flavor, which adds a spike of mild heat. Ground coriander imparts its brightness, the buttered bread crumbs add just enough richness to give the soup some decadence, and the crunch is the perfect foil to the soup's silky texture.

SERVES 6

- 1 baguette or 1 cup store-bought bread crumbs
- 2 tablespoons unsalted butter
- 3 teaspoons olive oil
- 1½ teaspoons ground white pepper
- 1 cup roughly chopped shallots
- 1 russet potato, peeled and chopped into 1-inch cubes
- 1½ tablespoons ground turmeric
- 1 teaspoon coriander seed, ground
- 1 teaspoon chile flakes
- 1 teaspoon cumin seed, ground
- 4 cups frozen sweet peas
- 1 quart chicken stock, plus more to taste
- 1 teaspoon kosher salt

1 | To prepare the bread crumbs, grate the baguette on a cheese grater, chop it small, or place in a food processor. You should have about 1 cup bread crumbs. In a large nonstick pan over medium heat, add the butter, 1 teaspoon of the olive oil, and ½ teaspoon of the white pepper. Once the butter and oil are hot, add the bread crumbs and stir occasionally. Cook until the bread crumbs are crispy and golden, about 2 minutes. Set aside.

2 | In a wide pot over medium heat, add the remaining 2 teaspoons olive oil. Once the oil is hot, add the shallots, potato, turmeric, coriander, remaining 1 teaspoon white pepper, chile flakes, and cumin. Cook, stirring occasionally, until golden, about 10 minutes. Add the peas. Add the chicken stock and salt and bring to a boil. Turn down the heat to just below a simmer and cook, covered, for 15 minutes. Allow to cool, then puree in a blender until smooth. For a silky texture, pass the puree through a fine-mesh strainer using the back of a large spoon to push on the solids and extract all of the liquid. Make sure to taste the soup and add more chicken stock if needed to thin the soup to the desired consistency.

3 | Ladle the hot soup into bowls. Top with the bread crumbs and serve.

GINGER-SPICED CHICKEN TIKKA SANDWICH WITH CUMIN-TOMATO MAYO

The yogurt in this sensational sandwich almost pickles and cures the marinated chicken, while the tandoori crust keeps everything juicy inside. The bright yellow roasted peppers add crunch to the creaminess of the earthy, spicy tomato mayo, and the garam masala makes it magic. Refrain from devouring every bite on sight and savor this over a glass of cold wine or a beer.

SERVES 4

3 teaspoons ghee
1 tablespoon garam masala
1 tablespoon finely chopped ginger
1 tablespoon finely chopped garlic
1/3 cup plain yogurt
3 tablespoons tomato puree
1 pound skinless, boneless chicken breasts

Kosher salt
1/2 cup mayonnaise
1 teaspoon cumin seed, ground
1 red bell pepper, thinly sliced
1 cup thinly sliced yellow onions
1 teaspoon ground turmeric
4 naan or pita breads
1 cup fresh cilantro, roughly chopped

1 | In a small pan over medium-high heat, add 1 teaspoon of the ghee. Add the garam masala, ginger, and garlic and cook for 30 seconds (this will bring out the flavorful oils of the spices). Transfer to a medium bowl large enough for the chicken. Stir in the yogurt and 2 tablespoons of the tomato puree.

2 | Slice each chicken breast horizontally into 3 to 4 slices. Place in the yogurt mixture and coat thoroughly. Cover the bowl with plastic wrap and refrigerate for at least 6 hours or overnight.

3 | Wipe the marinade off the chicken. Discard the marinade. Season the chicken with salt. In a large nonstick skillet over medium-high heat, add 1 teaspoon of the remaining ghee. Once the ghee is hot, sauté the chicken until golden on both sides, about 2 minutes per side. Set aside.

4 | In a small bowl, mix together the mayonnaise, the remaining 1 tablespoon tomato puree, and the cumin. Set aside.

continued

5 | In a medium nonstick skillet over medium-high heat, add the remaining 1 teaspoon ghee. Once the ghee is hot, add the red bell pepper, onions, and turmeric. Sprinkle with salt. Sauté until golden, about 3 minutes. Remove from the heat.

6 | Spread the bread with the mayonnaise mixture (if using pita, split it open). Add the chicken, then the peppers and onions mixture. Garnish with the cilantro. Serve immediately.

CRISPY CHEESE AND SWEET PEAS IN INDIAN-SPICED TOMATO SAUCE

This savory dish, popular in north India, usually features paneer, a classic mild cow's milk cheese (like ricotta), often used in desserts. In my global kitchen twist, I exchange paneer for Halloumi cheese (sheep's or goat's milk), which lends a mozzarella-like tang and gets deep, golden brown and soft but does not melt. (You can also use kasseri, a Greek frying cheese, for this same effect.)

SERVES 4

9 ounces Halloumi cheese	2 teaspoons finely chopped ginger
1 cup all-purpose flour	½ teaspoon chile flakes
2 tablespoons ghee, or 1 tablespoon unsalted butter and 1 tablespoon canola oil	2 cups tomato puree (see Flavor Secrets, opposite)
½ teaspoon cumin seed	1½ teaspoons kosher salt
½ teaspoon coriander seed	½ cup frozen peas
1 cup finely diced yellow onions	1 teaspoon garam masala
1 teaspoon ground turmeric	4 naan or pita breads, toasted

1 | Slice the Halloumi cheese into pieces that are 1 inch long and ⅓ inch thick. Dust in the flour and shake off the excess.

2 | In a wide nonstick skillet over medium heat, add 1 tablespoon of the ghee, or 1½ teaspoons of the butter and 1½ teaspoons of the canola oil. Once the ghee is melted and hot, add the Halloumi (be careful not to crowd the pan; do it in two batches if necessary). Cook the Halloumi until golden on both sides, about 2 minutes per side. Transfer to a plate and set aside.

3 | Grind the cumin and coriander together in a spice grinder to fine.

4 | Add the remaining 1 tablespoon ghee, or the remaining 1½ teaspoons butter and 1½ teaspoons canola oil, to the skillet and melt. Add the onions, turmeric, ground cumin and coriander, the ginger, and chile flakes and cook until deep golden, about 3 minutes.

5 | Add the tomato puree and salt and bring to a boil. Turn down the heat to low and cook for 15 minutes. Add the peas, the reserved Halloumi, and the garam masala and cook for 1 more minute.

6 | Spoon onto plates and serve with toasted naan or pita breads. Also great with basmati rice (see page 162).

FLAVOR SECRETS

If you use canned whole plum tomatoes or chopped tomatoes (high quality and with as few additional ingredients as possible), puree the tomatoes *with* their liquid in a food processor and use this as your tomato puree. If you use a regular store-bought tomato sauce, thin it out with water so that it's not too thick.

TURMERIC GRILLED SCALLOP PITAS

I've been in love with scallops ever since I worked at a fish company on San Francisco's Fisherman's Wharf. Scallops sear like steaks, yet their flesh retains a tender, lobsterlike quality. In this recipe, golden seared scallops are wrapped in pita bread. Visually it looks Middle Eastern, but the warm, mustardy sweet/savory flavor profile makes it clearly Indian, with mildly spicy yogurt. This is all about textures, spice, and comfort wrapped in little pockets of deliciousness.

SERVES 2

1 tablespoon canola oil, plus more for drizzling and rubbing	8 sea scallops
1 tablespoon finely chopped ginger	½ cup roasted, peeled, seeded, and chopped red bell pepper
1 teaspoon cumin seed, toasted and ground	¼ cup apple cider vinegar
½ teaspoon coriander seed, ground	¼ cup sugar
1 tablespoon ground turmeric	1 teaspoon kosher salt, plus more for seasoning
¾ cup plain yogurt	2 pita breads, cut in half
	½ cup fresh cilantro, large stems removed

1 | In a small skillet over medium heat, add the canola oil. Once the oil is hot, add the ginger, cumin, coriander, and turmeric and turn off the heat. Toast for 30 seconds. Using a rubber spatula, transfer the mixture to a bowl. Mix in ¼ cup of the yogurt. Add the scallops and coat well. Place in the refrigerator to marinate for at least 1 hour or up to 24 hours before using.

2 | In a small sauté pan over medium-high heat, add the red bell peppers, vinegar, and sugar and a pinch of the salt. Bring to a boil and simmer until a saucelike consistency forms, about 5 minutes. Remove from the heat. Let cool.

3 | Remove the scallops from the marinade and discard the marinade. Using your fingers, wipe off the excess marinade and set the scallops on a dry plate. Season the scallops with the salt. Drizzle a touch of canola oil on the scallops to prevent sticking.

continued

4 | Preheat the grill to medium-high. Rub the grill with a touch of canola oil. Sear the scallops on the grill for about 2 minutes on each side, until cooked. While the scallops are grilling, you can grill the pitas for about 30 seconds on each side, just to warm and soften them.

5 | To assemble, chop the scallops into ½-inch pieces. Lay the pitas on a platter or individual plates. Fill the pitas evenly with the chopped scallops and cilantro. Add the remaining yogurt and the bell pepper mixture.

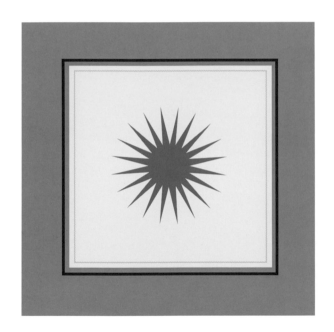

THREE-SPICE SHRIMP ON CURRIED YELLOW SPLIT PEAS

Being a fan of Mexican food makes me an instant fan of Indian food. Both cuisines share common spices like cumin and coriander, and flavor profiles that intensify and change when mixed with other spices. Indian cooking is a great way to get huge flavor without heavy eating.

MAKES 6 APPETIZERS

½ cup yellow split peas

1 teaspoon unsalted butter

3 teaspoons canola oil

¼ cup finely chopped yellow onion

1½ teaspoons curry powder

2 cups water

½ teaspoon kosher salt, plus more for seasoning

1 teaspoon cumin seed

1 teaspoon coriander seed

1 teaspoon chile flakes

18 jumbo shrimp, tails on, peeled and deveined

3 tablespoons chopped fresh cilantro

1 | Place the dry split peas in a medium bowl and fill with cold water. Pour off any debris that floats to the surface. Look through the peas to make sure there are no pebbles. Pour the split peas into a strainer and set aside to drain.

2 | In a small pot over medium heat, add the butter and 1 teaspoon of the canola oil. Once the butter and oil are hot, add the onion. Cook, stirring occasionally, until the onion is soft and golden, about 4 minutes. Add the curry powder and stir. Cook for 1 minute. Add the water and split peas and bring to a boil. Turn down the heat to low and cover the pot. Keep an eye on the split peas. You want them to cook until tender but still hold their shape—about 35 minutes. Once the split peas are tender, add the salt. If you add it before they're soft, the salt will prevent the split peas from getting tender.

3 | When the split peas have about 10 minutes' cooking time left, prepare the shrimp. Grind the cumin, coriander, and chile flakes together in a spice grinder or coffee grinder to a sandy consistency. Toss the shrimp in the spice blend. Season with salt.

continued

4 | In a large skillet over medium-high heat, add the remaining 2 teaspoons canola oil. Use a large enough skillet to provide about 1½ inches of space between the shrimp to nicely brown. (If too crowded in the pan, the shrimp will steam instead of brown.) Once the oil is hot, add the shrimp. (You may have to do this in two batches, depending on the size of your pan.) Sear to a deep golden on the first side, then flip the shrimp to finish cooking. Watch the sides of the shrimp. When they go from clear and raw looking to opaque, they are done. The shrimp will continue to cook a little when removed from the pan, so pull them out as soon as you see the sides turn opaque. If the shrimp feel too hard or start to curl, they are overcooked.

5 | To serve, place a spoonful of split peas on each serving plate and spread them out thinly. Top each plate with 3 shrimp, browned sides up. Garnish with the cilantro and serve.

TANDOORI-STYLE CHICKEN WITH BASMATI RICE AND SPICY TOMATO CHUTNEY

Cumin leaves Mexico and heads to India in this popular dish, where thin pieces of juicy chicken and sweet, tangy tomato chutney come together with the mustardy heat of turmeric and the perfume of toasted coriander.

SERVES 4

5 teaspoons ghee or canola oil	1 teaspoon finely chopped serrano chile or red chile of your choice
1 tablespoon garam masala	2½ teaspoons kosher salt, plus more for seasoning
1 tablespoon finely chopped ginger	Freshly ground black pepper
1 tablespoon finely chopped garlic	2 cups basmati rice
1 teaspoon cumin seed	3 cups water
½ cup plain yogurt	1½ teaspoons ground turmeric
4 skin-on, bone-in chicken breasts	1 tablespoon olive oil
½ teaspoon coriander seed, ground	1 red bell pepper, thinly sliced
¼ cup sugar	1 cup thinly sliced yellow onions
¼ cup red wine vinegar	¼ cup fresh cilantro, roughly chopped
1 cup diced tomatoes	4 naan or pita breads

1 | In a small pan over medium-high heat, add 2 teaspoons of the ghee. Add the garam masala, ginger, garlic, and cumin seed and cook for 30 seconds. Transfer to a bowl that's large enough for the chicken. Stir in the yogurt.

2 | Place the chicken in the yogurt mixture and stir to coat thoroughly. Cover the bowl with plastic wrap and chill in the refrigerator for at least 6 hours or overnight.

3 | To prepare the chutney, in a small skillet over medium heat, add the coriander and toast just until you can smell it, about 2 minutes. Add the sugar and vinegar and stir until the sugar is dissolved. Stir in the tomatoes, chile, and ½ teaspoon of the salt. Bring to a boil, turn down the heat, and cook at a very low simmer until you have a thick, saucy consistency, about 5 minutes.

continued

Remember that the chutney will thicken as it cools, so it should look a little thinner when hot. Transfer to a small condiment serving dish. (You can make this up to 3 days ahead and store in a covered container in the refrigerator. Bring to room temperature before serving.)

4 | When ready to cook the chicken, preheat the oven to 375°F.

5 | Remove the chicken from the yogurt marinade and wipe off all the yogurt. Discard the marinade. Season the chicken with salt and black pepper. Allow the chicken to come to room temperature before cooking.

6 | In a medium ovenproof skillet over medium-high heat, add 2 teaspoons of the remaining ghee. Once the ghee is hot, place the chicken, skin side down, in the pan. Sauté until golden, about 3 minutes, and then flip over the chicken and cook for another 3 minutes. Remove from the heat. Carefully transfer the skillet to the oven. Cook until a meat thermometer reads 150°F in the thickest part of the chicken. If you don't have a thermometer, cut into the chicken and peek.

7 | Remove the skillet from the oven and let sit for 15 minutes. The residual heat from the skillet will continue to cook the chicken—be sure it's 160°F before serving.

8 | To prepare the basmati rice, in a medium pot, add the rice. Rinse with cold water, then pour out the water and leave the wet rice. (This removes a layer of starch so that the rice is not sticky.) Add the water, ½ teaspoon of the turmeric, the remaining 2 teaspoons salt, and the olive oil. Stir together and bring to a boil. Turn down the heat to low and cover the pot. Cook until all the water is absorbed and the rice is tender but still has body, 20 to 25 minutes. Leave the pot uncovered for about 10 minutes to let out the excess heat, then cover it back up until ready to serve.

9 | In a medium nonstick skillet over medium-high heat, add the remaining 1 teaspoon ghee. Once the ghee is hot, add the red bell pepper, onions, and the remaining 1 teaspoon turmeric. Sprinkle with salt to taste. Sauté until golden, about 5 minutes. Spread out on a serving platter.

10| Place the chicken on top of the onion mixture. Garnish with the cilantro. Serve the tomato chutney, basmati rice, and naan on the side.

GARAM MASALA CHICKEN POT PIE

This may look like a typical American chicken pot pie, but culinary rock star garam masala transforms it into a serious soul-warming Indian delight. Tender chunks of chicken and the flaky pastry crust on top round out the recipe with toasty warmth and tons of additional flavor from garam masala's cumin, cardamom, and sweet baking spices. Using frozen puff pastry makes this dish super easy.

SERVES 4

4   skinless, boneless chicken thighs

2   teaspoons kosher salt, plus more for seasoning

    Freshly ground black pepper

2   tablespoons olive oil

2   garlic cloves, finely chopped

2   shallots, chopped

1   carrot, sliced ⅓ inch thick

2   tablespoons salted butter

3   tablespoons all-purpose flour, plus more for dusting

3   cups chicken stock

1   russet potato, peeled and cut into ½-inch cubes

½   cup heavy cream

½   cup frozen peas, defrosted

1½   tablespoons garam masala, plus more for sprinkling

One   1-pound package (2 sheets) frozen puff pastry, defrosted slightly

1 | Preheat the oven to 400°F.

2 | Season the chicken with salt and pepper. In a medium pot over medium-high heat, add the olive oil. Brown the chicken on both sides until golden, about 5 minutes on each side. Remove the chicken from the pot to a cutting board and set aside.

3 | To the same pot, add the garlic, shallots, and carrot and sauté until golden, about 4 minutes. Remove the carrot mixture to a bowl and set aside. Turn down the heat to medium.

4 | Melt the butter in the pot, whisk in the flour, and cook for 1 minute. Stir in the chicken stock and whisk until smooth. Add the potatoes and cook until the potatoes are mostly cooked but still firm, 8 to 10 minutes. Stir in the cream. The chicken stock will have thickened to a sauce consistency. Remove from the heat.

continued

5 | Chop the chicken into ¾-inch chunks and add the chicken and carrot mixture back to the pot. Stir in the peas, garam masala, and 2 teaspoons salt. Ladle the mixture into four 10-ounce ovenproof bowls.

6 | On a flat work surface, dust the puff pastry with flour and roll it out just a little thinner than it comes. Cut the puff pastry into squares large enough to hang over the sides of each bowl. Cover the bowls with the puff pastry, pressing down around the sides to seal. Put the bowls on a baking sheet, transfer it to the oven, and bake until the tops are golden brown, about 15 minutes.

WHOLE TANDOORI CHICKEN WITH MUSTARD SEED—ROASTED POTATOES

Not your ordinary chicken here. Normally chicken doesn't look good until it's dark and roasted. This one looks fantastic even when it's raw because it's rubbed with beautiful, bright yellow turmeric. The yogurt tenderizes the meat and adds heft to the flavor profiles of turmeric, cumin, and black pepper. The potatoes are roasted in brown mustard seeds that add just enough heat and crunch to the creamy chunks. Once the whole thing is hot and roasted, the chicken is tender and falling off the bone, and your kitchen will smell like a warm Indian spice garden.

SERVES 4

1 teaspoon cumin seed	2 tablespoons ghee or unsalted butter
½ teaspoon fenugreek (optional)	1 chicken (3 to 4 pounds)
1 teaspoon coriander seed	3 cups chopped fingerling potatoes (½-inch cubes)
1 teaspoon freshly ground black pepper	2 teaspoons canola oil
1 tablespoon ground turmeric	2 teaspoons whole brown mustard seeds
1 tablespoon kosher salt, plus more for seasoning	

1 | Preheat the oven to 325°F.

2 | Grind together the cumin, fenugreek (if using), coriander, and black pepper in a spice grinder or coffee grinder. Move to a small bowl, and mix in the turmeric and salt. Mix in the ghee to form a seasoned paste. Rub all over the chicken, including under its skin.

3 | Place the chicken on a rack in a roasting pan. Tie together the wings and legs and place in the oven. Roast until the internal temperature at the thickest part of the breast and leg is 150°F. Remove from the oven and let sit for 15 minutes.

4 | While the chicken is roasting, add the potatoes to a medium pot and cover with water. Boil until tender, about 8 minutes. Drain and rinse under cold water. Pat dry with a paper towel. In a medium nonstick skillet over medium-high heat, add the canola oil. Once the oil is hot, add the potatoes and mustard seeds and stir occasionally until golden brown. Season with salt.

5 | Place the chicken on a platter and garnish with the potatoes. Serve.

MELTING POT AMERICA

...

America is called a melting pot for a reason. Every world cuisine has touched our shores and embedded itself so deeply into our fare that, aside from apple pie and hamburgers, most of us have to stop and ask, What *is* American food, anyway?

A Lebanese boy raised in Chicago, I'm a culinary hybrid. I grew up a huge fan, in equal measure, of burgers and bulgur, shrimp cocktails and *sfeeha*. My life and my cooking have always been about transcending borders, and the recipes in this chapter reflect that sensibility, from the BLT with Oven-Dried Tomatoes and Harissa Mayo (page 188) to the Smoked Paprika Buttermilk Fried Chicken (page 182). They're among my "American" favorites, inspired by my mind-tasting travels around the world.

ALL SPICES OF THE WORLD HAPPILY COEXIST IN

OUR AMERICAN MELTING POT,

AND EACH FLAVOR PROFILED IN THIS BOOK FINDS ITS WAY

INTO THE RECIPES IN THIS CHAPTER.

AMERICAN FLAVOR FAMILY

GRILLED RADICCHIO WITH BALSAMIC VINEGAR, PARMESAN, AND SEA SALT

Radicchio is one of my favorite vegetables. It's like endive's French or Italian cousin: beautiful, appealingly bitter, and sensational rubbed with a little bit of olive oil, grilled, and drizzled with balsamic vinegar. I love the way this bitter red green wilts, chars, and mellows on the grill in a matter of minutes. The sharp-sweet balsamic drizzle is the perfect balance with the salty, nutty cheese, creating a perfect summer side with grilled fish or chicken.

SERVES 4

- 2 heads Treviso or 4 heads round radicchio
- 1 teaspoon olive oil
- ½ cup balsamic vinegar
- ¼ teaspoon chile flakes or to taste (optional)
- ½ cup shaved Parmesan cheese
- Pinch of sea salt

1 | Preheat a grill to high.

2 | Peel the leaves off the Treviso and lay them on a plate. Rub with the olive oil.

3 | In a saucepan over high heat, add the balsamic vinegar. Reduce the vinegar by half. (If you like spice, add a sprinkle of chile flakes to the reducing balsamic.) This concentrates the flavor and makes the vinegar sweeter and thicker. Set aside to cool.

4 | Lay the leaves on the hot grill. Monitor closely as it takes only 1 minute for them to wilt and char. Flip over and cook briefly, about another 30 seconds. Lay the leaves on a platter. Drizzle with the balsamic, spread the Parmesan over evenly, and sprinkle with a touch of sea salt. Serve immediately.

BRUSSELS SPROUTS HASH WITH TOASTED CORIANDER

Brussels sprouts get a bum rap because they're often cooked into a bitter, boiled cabbage state (sorry, Mom!). Nothing like that here. These small veggie wonders are caramelized, sweet, and heightened by the bright citrus note of coriander. They're like hash browns without the potatoes—a green, golden savory delight that even your kids will love. This hash makes a great appetizer or side dish—just add a couple of poached or fried eggs on top.

SERVES 4

3 cups Brussels sprouts

3 ounces pancetta or bacon, roughly chopped

1 tablespoon olive oil

½ teaspoon freshly ground black pepper

½ teaspoon coriander seed, ground

1 cup thinly sliced red onions

¼ cup chicken stock

Pinch of kosher salt

1 | Cut the ends off of the Brussels sprouts and then cut the Brussels sprouts in half. Discard the end pieces and the first layer of leaves, if discolored. Shred thin.

2 | Heat a large sauté pan over medium-high heat. Add the pancetta and cook for about 3 minutes, until golden. Drain off the fat and discard. Add the olive oil to the pan. Add the pepper and coriander and cook for 30 seconds to toast the spices.

3 | Add the Brussels sprouts and red onions to the pan and cook until deep golden and slightly crispy, 6 to 8 minutes. Add the chicken stock and salt and stir. Cook for 1 more minute. The stock will be gone, but it will leave the mixture moist but still roasted.

CUMIN-RUBBED SHRIMP COCKTAIL WITH THREE-CHILE-SPICED SAUCE

The first shrimp cocktail I ate was an epiphany: such tiny objects, such big flavor! I was bowled over by those plump pink crustaceans hanging off the rim of the glass and by the mysterious red sauce in the middle, with its intense wasabi-ginger burn of horseradish and pepper. This recipe is an ode to that moment, with a Latin twist.

SERVES 4 TO 8

SAUCE

- 1 medium yellow onion, cut into quarters
- 1 jalapeño chile
- 1 serrano chile
- 1 tablespoon canola oil
- 1 tablespoon roughly chopped garlic
- ½ teaspoon finely diced orange habanero chile
- 2 cups tomato puree
- 1 teaspoon soy sauce
- 1 tablespoon agave syrup
- 2 tablespoons apple cider vinegar
- 1 teaspoon kosher salt
  Pinch of ground cinnamon

SHRIMP

- 1 teaspoon cumin seed
- 1 teaspoon coriander seed
- ½ teaspoon freshly ground black pepper
- 2 pounds jumbo shrimp, tails on, peeled and deveined
- 1 tablespoon canola oil
- 1 tablespoon roughly chopped fresh cilantro

1 | First, prepare the sauce. Heat a grill to high or place a grill pan over high heat on the stove.

2 | Place the onion, jalapeño, and serrano chile on the grill. Grill until slightly charred, about 5 minutes. Set aside to cool. (You can pan-roast the onion, jalapeño, and serrano if you don't want to grill.)

3 | Once they have cooled, cut the jalapeño and the serrano in half and remove the stems and seeds. Leave in more seeds for more heat.

4 | In a medium pot over medium heat, add the canola oil. Once the oil is hot, add the grilled onion and chiles and the garlic, habanero chile, tomato puree, soy sauce, agave syrup, vinegar, salt, and cinnamon. Bring to a boil, then turn down to low and cover. Cook for 30 minutes. Allow to cool. Once cool, puree in a blender until smooth. Chill in the refrigerator overnight.

5 | When you are ready to cook the shrimp, preheat the oven to 400°F.

6 | In a dry skillet over medium heat, toast the cumin, coriander, and black pepper just until you can smell them. Pour into a bowl and allow to cool for a couple of minutes. Grind in a spice grinder or coffee grinder to a sandlike consistency.

7 | Toss the shrimp in a bowl with the spices and the canola oil to coat evenly. Lay the shrimp evenly on a sheet pan (do not crowd the shrimp or they will steam instead of browning).

8 | Place the sheet pan in the oven and cook until the shrimp turn from translucent to opaque and white. Keep in mind that they will continue to cook a little more when you remove them from the oven. Don't hesitate to cut one open and check.

9 | Allow to cool for 15 minutes. Place in a covered container and refrigerate until very cold. Serve on a platter with the cocktail sauce in the center for dipping. You can also serve by placing 3 to 5 shrimp over the edge of a martini-style glass with the cocktail sauce in the center. Garnish with the fresh cilantro.

STEAK SALAD WITH ALMOND-BASIL DRESSING

A perfect balance of seared steak and light salad, dressed with my global kitchen version of green goddess, which is a marriage of basil and toasted almonds.

SERVES 4

¼ cup skinless slivered almonds
½ cup fresh basil
1 tablespoon fresh lemon juice
2 tablespoons red wine vinegar
2 tablespoons buttermilk
½ cup plus 3 tablespoons olive oil

½ teaspoon kosher salt, plus more for seasoning
16 cups arugula, washed and dried
1 cup Bush's Best cannellini beans, rinsed and drained
12 ounces flank steak
Freshly ground black pepper

1 | Toast the almonds in a dry skillet over medium heat until golden, about 3 minutes. Set aside to cool.

2 | In a food processor, add the almonds, basil, lemon juice, vinegar, buttermilk, ½ cup plus 2 tablespoons of the olive oil, and the salt. Puree until smooth.

3 | In a large bowl, toss the arugula with ¾ cup of the pureed dressing. Taste and adjust per your taste if you like more dressing. (It's always better to start with less dressing as you can always add more, but you can't take it away.)

4 | Divide the arugula among four plates or heap on a platter. Spread the beans evenly across the arugula.

5 | To prepare the steak, pat it dry with a paper towel and season with salt and pepper.

6 | In a medium skillet over medium-high heat, add the remaining 1 tablespoon olive oil. Once the oil is hot (just starts to haze), add the steak. Sear until deep golden, about 3 minutes per side. Flip the steak and cook until the internal temperature at the thickest part is 120°F (for medium-rare). Set aside to cool.

7 | Once the steak is cool, cut into ½-inch-thick slices. Place on top of the salad and serve.

FLAVOR SECRETS

Cut steak lengthwise against the grain and on a 45-degree angle. This shortens the tough muscle fibers and connective tissues and yields more tender slices of steak.

TOASTED CORIANDER CHICKEN NOODLE SOUP

Chicken noodle soup is the most comforting and classic soup around. This one is perfumed with toasted ground coriander to warm your soul. You can use dark meat if you want a richer soup. Like Grandma used to make it—only better.

SERVES 4

1 tablespoon unsalted butter	1 cup thickly sliced celery
1 tablespoon olive oil	1 teaspoon coriander seed, ground
One 5-ounce skinless, boneless chicken breast (skin on optional)	2 bay leaves, finely ground
½ teaspoon kosher salt, plus more for seasoning	5 cups chicken stock
Freshly ground black pepper	1 teaspoon finely chopped fresh thyme
2 cups thinly sliced yellow onions	2 ounces spaghetti
1 cup sliced carrots (⅓ inch thick)	Zest of 1 lemon
	2 tablespoons roughly chopped fresh flat-leaf parsley

1 | In a pot over medium heat, add the butter and olive oil.

2 | Season the chicken breast with salt and pepper and place in the middle of the pot. Add the onions, carrots, and celery around the chicken. Cook, stirring occasionally, for about 6 minutes, until the chicken and veggies are golden on both sides. Add the coriander and bay leaves and stir to toast briefly. Add the chicken stock, thyme, and ½ teaspoon salt and bring to a boil. Remove the chicken and set on a plate to cool. If you used skin-on chicken, remove the skin now and discard. (Skin on the chicken will result in more fat/flavor as you sauté the chicken.)

3 | Add the spaghetti to the pot and cook until al dente. Turn off the heat, leaving the spaghetti in the soup. Add the lemon zest.

4 | Once it is cool, shred the chicken breast with two forks and add the meat back into the soup.

5 | Ladle the soup into four bowls. Garnish each with some of the chopped parsley.

GROVE'S BOURBON, BACON, ALLSPICE CHILI

I created this chili for the Grove restaurants in San Francisco, and it's been a hit ever since. The cocoa, bourbon, bacon, and spices come together to create a deep, rustic, chili. For even more flavor contrasts, top it with a bit of sour cream, shredded Jack cheese, and finely chopped green onions. This chili is great for families or parties, and perfect paired with a robust red wine or a beer.

SERVES 5 TO 7

1 teaspoon cumin seed	8 ounces ground beef (15% fat)
1 teaspoon dried Mexican oregano	8 ounces ground pork
⅛ teaspoon ground allspice	¼ cup bourbon
¼ teaspoon ground cinnamon	2 tablespoons tomato paste
1 star anise pod	1½ cups tomato puree or sauce
½ teaspoon chile flakes	3 cups beef stock
1 tablespoon mixed ground guajillo and ancho chiles or 1 tablespoon chili powder	One 15-ounce can Bush's Best kidney beans, rinsed and drained
1 teaspoon canola oil	One 15-ounce can Bush's Best pinto beans, rinsed and drained
2 ounces bacon, roughly chopped	½ teaspoon unsweetened cocoa powder
1 tablespoon roughly chopped garlic	Sour cream (optional)
1 cup roughly chopped yellow onions	Shredded Jack or cheddar cheese (optional)
½ cup roughly chopped carrots	Finely chopped green onions (optional)
1½ teaspoons kosher salt	

1 | Put the cumin, oregano, allspice, cinnamon, star anise, chile flakes, and guajillo and ancho chiles in a spice grinder or coffee grinder and grind to a fine, sandy consistency.

2 | In a medium pot over medium heat, add the canola oil and bacon. Cook until the bacon is golden, about 3 minutes. Add the garlic, onions, and carrots and cook until golden, about 3 minutes. Add the spice mixture and salt and cook for 1 minute to toast the spices.

3 | Immediately add the beef and pork and break apart into small pieces. Cook until deep golden, about 15 minutes. Make a hole in the center so you can see the bottom of the pan and add the bourbon. Stir to pick up all the brown bits on the bottom of the pan. The bourbon will disappear almost instantly. Let the mixture cook for 1 minute to burn off the alcohol.

4 | Add the tomato paste, tomato puree, beef stock, kidney beans, pinto beans, and cocoa powder and bring to a boil. Simmer, uncovered, for 5 minutes, then cover, turn down the heat to low, and cook for 20 minutes.

5 | Ladle the chili into bowls and serve immediately as is, or garnish with the desired amounts of sour cream, shredded Jack or cheddar cheese, and green onions.

LOBSTER POT PIE WITH FAVA BEANS, TARRAGON, AND CORIANDER BUTTER CRUST

Pot pies are the ultimate comfort food and were one of my childhood favorite dishes: tender veggies and rich broth under a flaky, buttery layer of golden pastry dough. This delicious variation on a theme has chunks of lobster, the citrus-anise perfume of tarragon, and the creamy mild green bean flavor of fava beans.

SERVES 4

One 1-pound package (2 sheets) frozen puff pastry

1 cup chopped fingerling potatoes (½-inch cubes)

1 cup shelled and skinned fava beans

1½ tablespoons olive oil

1 celery stalk, chopped

½ cup sliced carrots (⅓ inch thick)

1 tablespoon finely chopped garlic

½ cup finely chopped shallots

3 tablespoons unsalted butter

3 tablespoons all-purpose flour, plus more for dusting

½ cup dry white wine

1½ quarts fish stock or vegetable stock

12 ounces cooked lobster, cut into ½-inch pieces

½ cup fresh tarragon, roughly chopped (set aside 2 tablespoons for garnish)

1½ teaspoons kosher salt

2 large eggs

1 | Preheat the oven to 400°F.

2 | Pull the puff pastry out of the freezer and set on a counter.

3 | Bring a medium pot of water to a boil. Add the cubed potatoes and cook until still slightly firm (they can easily be cut with a fork but they don't fall apart). Drain and cool under running water to stop the cooking. Set aside.

4 | Bring a medium saucepan of water to a simmer over medium heat. Add the fava beans and cook until tender, about 3 minutes. Immediately run under cold water to stop the cooking. Set aside.

5 | In a medium pot over medium heat, add the olive oil. Add the celery and carrots and cook just until soft but not browned. Add the garlic and shallots, and cook for 1 more minute. Do not brown the garlic. Remove all the veggies from the pot and set aside.

6 | Add the butter to the same pot. Once the butter is melted, whisk in the flour and cook for 30 seconds while whisking to avoid any lumps. Whisk in the white wine. Boil for 1 minute to remove most of the alcohol and concentrate the wine flavor. Add the fish stock and bring to a boil, whisking occasionally. Simmer until the liquid has a saucelike consistency. You do not want it to be watery or pasty. It should be like a creamy soup.

7 | Add the potatoes, fava beans, and cooked celery mixture to the pot and turn off the heat. Stir in the lobster, tarragon (less 2 tablespoons), and salt. The potatoes, veggies, and lobster will cook further in the oven when you are cooking them with the puff pastry on top.

8 | Ladle the filling mixture evenly into four 8-ounce ramekins or ovenproof bowls. Leave at least 1 inch of space from the top of the rim so that the puff pastry does not touch the liquid. Set the ramekins on a sheet pan so that you can easily get them in and out of the oven.

9 | Dust the puff pastry with flour and roll out to just a little thinner than it comes. (The dough should be very cold so it rises nicely in the oven.) Use the ramekins as your gauge. You want the pastry to be about 2 inches wider than the size of the ramekin. Cut each of the 2 rolled-out pieces in half on a diagonal. Gently stretch each piece of pastry over the top of a ramekin and gently press it around the edges to seal it. Allow the dough to hang over the sides a bit; trim slightly if necessary. It will yield a rustic look and some beautiful golden brown triangles of crust to tear off and dip into your filling.

10| Whisk the eggs in a small bowl. Brush the pastry tops with the whisked eggs. Bake the pot pies in the oven for 15 minutes, or until the tops are golden brown and puffed. Place each ramekin on a plate with a liner (to avoid sliding) and garnish the tops with the remaining 2 tablespoons chopped tarragon.

SMOKED PAPRIKA BUTTERMILK FRIED CHICKEN

Who doesn't love fried chicken? I fell in love with this classic comfort food again while shooting the fried chicken episode for *United Tastes of America* on the Cooking Channel. I was lucky enough to cook chicken with the best chefs across the country. The combination of spices in this recipe yields a full-flavored chicken, and the brine makes it super moist. This chicken is best served on a bun as a sandwich or as a main course with sautéed kale.

SERVES 4

2 cups all-purpose flour

2 tablespoons cumin seed, ground

2 tablespoons freshly ground black pepper

2 tablespoons smoked paprika

1 pound boneless (with or without skin) chicken breasts, brined (see Flavor Secrets, page 66)

1 pound boneless (with or without skin) chicken thighs, brined (see Flavor Secrets, page 66)

6 to 8 cups canola oil

2 cups buttermilk

1 | In a medium bowl, mix together the flour, cumin, pepper, and paprika. Stir with a whisk or fork to combine well. Set aside.

2 | Remove the chicken from the brine and rinse in cold water. Pat dry with a paper towel.

3 | In a fryer or deep pot over medium-high heat, add canola oil at least 6 inches deep. Heat the oil to 340°F (use a frying thermometer to check). Everything is time-sensitive and performed with very high heat, so organization is critical. While the oil is heating, arrange the following items on your countertop in order: plate with the dry chicken; bowl with the seasoned flour; bowl with the buttermilk; slotted spoon; wire cooling rack set over a sheet pan or heat-resistant platter. Make sure the oil is hot enough and everything is lined up and ready to go. It's important that the chicken goes from the flour directly into the oil without sitting.

4 | Once the oil reaches 340°F, pick up the chicken pieces one by one. Coat each in flour and shake off the excess. Dip each into the buttermilk and allow the excess to drip off. Dredge in the flour again and shake off the excess. Once you have 4 to 5 pieces ready, carefully release the chicken

into the oil. Cook pieces that are of similar size in the same batch. Cook until deep golden brown, about 7 minutes. Use a slotted spoon to remove the chicken to the wire rack. Let the chicken rest. Once it is cool enough to handle, cut into a piece to make sure it's cooked all the way through. Cooking times will vary based on the oil temperature and the size of the pieces.

5 | Serve immediately.

Sautéed Kale with Walnut Oil, Lemon Juice, and Chile Flakes

Wash 2 bunches of kale and spin dry. Remove the large stems and discard. Chop the leaves and the remaining small stems into 2-inch pieces. In a large sauté pan over high heat, add 2 tablespoons walnut oil. Once the oil is hot, add ¼ teaspoon chile flakes and the kale. Using tongs, keep the kale moving as if you were stir-frying. Add a pinch of kosher salt. Stop sautéing as soon as the kale wilts but still has body—not quite as soft as sautéed spinach. Once the kale is wilted, add 2 tablespoons fresh lemon juice and mix well. Transfer to a serving dish or to individual side-dish plates. Using a Microplane or grater, zest 1 lemon over the top for a little golden color and a citrus bite. Serve immediately.

GRILLED CHICKEN WITH TARRAGON-ROASTED TOMATOES

The tarragon makes this dish French, the orzo makes it Italian, and chicken makes it a tasty family classic. I love orzo because it eats like rice but it has the body of a pasta or risotto. (In fact, whatever you can do with risotto, you can do with orzo.)

SERVES 4

4	skinless, boneless chicken breasts
2	cups cherry tomatoes
1	tablespoon olive oil, plus more for rubbing
	Pinch of chile flakes

	Kosher salt and freshly ground black pepper
1/3	cup fresh tarragon
1/2	cup orzo
1/4	cup grated Parmesan cheese
1	tablespoon unsalted butter

1 | Preheat a grill to medium-high.

2 | Place the chicken breasts one at a time in a large plastic bag or inside a large folded piece of plastic wrap. Using a food mallet or the bottom of a sauté pan, pound the chicken firmly and evenly to 1/3-inch thickness, being careful not to tear the meat. Set aside.

3 | Rinse the tomatoes and pull off their stems. Pat dry with a paper towel. Take a large piece of aluminum foil and double it over with the shiny side up. Place the whole tomatoes in the center. Pour the olive oil evenly over them. Add the chile flakes and season with salt and pepper. Pull the tarragon leaves off the stems and place on the tomatoes. Close up the foil to create a pouch. Place the pouch of tomatoes on the hot side of the grill.

4 | Season the chicken breasts with salt and pepper and rub with a touch of olive oil. Cook on the hot side of the grill until you have nice grill marks, about 2 minutes. Rotate the chicken breasts 45 degrees and grill them until you have another set of grill marks, about 2 minutes. You will have that nice grill mark pattern. Flip over the chicken breasts and move them to the cool side of grill. Grill for about 2 minutes. When you touch the chicken breasts and they have a little give, they are done. If they feel very spongy, they are still undercooked. If they feel hard, they are hockey pucks. Remove from the grill and cover with aluminum foil. Let rest for 5 minutes.

continued

5 | While the chicken is grilling, prepare the orzo. Bring a medium pot of water with 2 teaspoons salt to a boil. Add the orzo and cook until al dente, about 10 minutes (taste for doneness). Remove the pot from the heat. Drain the orzo and return it to the pot. Stir in the Parmesan and butter.

6 | Spoon the orzo evenly on a large platter. Lay the chicken breasts across the orzo. Pour the roasted cherry tomatoes over the chicken. Serve immediately.

BLT WITH OVEN-DRIED TOMATOES AND HARISSA MAYO

The great American BLT is amped up with the flavors of North Africa and the sweet, sharp flavor of oven-dried tomatoes. There is so much going on in this sandwich: The process of oven drying transforms even the blandest tomato by concentrating flavors and intensifying both sweetness and acidity. The intensity comes together with the spiciness of the harissa; the smoky, salty flavor of bacon; and the crisp flourish of lettuce. One bite and you'll want to make ten more of these delicious sandwiches.

SERVES 4

3 ripe large Roma tomatoes	12 slices thick-cut high-quality bacon
1 tablespoon olive oil	8 slices thick-cut rustic bread
1 teaspoon caraway seeds, toasted and roughly ground	⅓ cup mayonnaise
Kosher salt	2 tablespoons harissa
	8 romaine lettuce leaves

1 | Preheat the oven to 275°F.

2 | Slice the tomatoes ½ inch thick.

3 | On a nonreactive sheet pan or in a large glass baking dish, pour the olive oil. Sprinkle with the caraway seeds and a touch of salt. Place the tomatoes in the oil and stir to coat. Spread them out evenly on the pan or in the dish. Place in the oven and bake for about 3 hours, or until they are about one-third of their original thickness. This creates a reduction by eliminating water and concentrating the sugars and essential tomato flavor. Some tomatoes will be slightly golden and others, which are toward the edges of the pan, may be slightly charred. Set aside to cool. (You can do a large batch of these several days ahead of time and keep them covered in the refrigerator. They are great for pasta sauces and sandwiches of any kind.)

4 | Preheat the oven to 400°F.

5 | Lay the bacon on a sheet pan and place in the oven. Cook the bacon to the desired doneness and remove from the oven. Drain on a paper towel.

6 | Toast the bread to golden.

7 | In a small bowl, mix together the mayonnaise and harissa. Spread 1 tablespoon of the harissa mayo on each slice of bread. On 4 of the slices, divide the bacon up evenly on the bread, then add the romaine, then the tomatoes. Place the other slice of bread on top. Cut the sandwiches in half and serve.

PROTEIN POWERHOUSE
EGGS

...

Open an egg carton and you have twelve sous-chefs at your fingertips. You can eat eggs for breakfast, lunch, or dinner. You can bake, fry, scramble, poach, or hard-cook them. There's barely a baked good on earth that doesn't love them.

Eggs are also the ultimate mind and body fuel. One egg is filled with high-quality protein, thirteen vitamins and minerals, and essential omega-3 fatty acids. They are fantastically delicious *and* a perfectly neutral vehicle for spices. Plus they're universally used and loved in every world cuisine around. Need I say more?

As a spokesperson for the American Egg Board, I am super proud to represent our country's egg industry and the Good Egg Project, which helps farmers and consumers feed the hungry. I blog about eggs on a regular basis, spreading the word about their beauty and bounty by demonstrating recipes like Harissa-Baked Eggs with Feta, Mint, and Black Olives (page 204) and Scrambled Eggs with Sautéed Pancetta, Radicchio, and Lemon (page 206). And I'm excited to share a few of those recipes—and some new ones—with you here.

THERE'S NOT AN HERB OR SPICE THAT

DOESN'T TASTE GREAT WITH EGGS.

EXPERIMENT WITH THE RECIPES IN THIS CHAPTER

AND SEE FOR YOURSELF.

EGG FLAVOR FAMILY

POACHED EGG AND ARUGULA BRUSCHETTA WITH TRUFFLE OIL AND SHAVED PARMESAN

Arugula is like spinach with attitude. Here, its peppery spice contrasts with the saltiness of Parmesan, the subtle depth of truffle oil, and the citrus burst of lemon zest. Truffle oil comes in black or white, and the most important thing when buying it is to look at the label to make sure there is at least a percentage of real truffle in the infused oil. Store it in the refrigerator to keep it fresh. Substitute olive oil if you prefer. Eat the bruschetta tapas style as an appetizer or as a meal.

SERVES 4

4 large slices rustic bread	4 large eggs
2 tablespoons plus 1 teaspoon olive oil	4 teaspoons truffle oil or extra virgin olive oil
2 garlic cloves	½ cup shaved Parmesan cheese
8 cups arugula, washed and dried	1 tablespoon roughly chopped fresh flat-leaf parsley
Kosher salt	Zest of 1 lemon, grated
1 tablespoon fresh lemon juice	
1 teaspoon red wine vinegar	

1 | Rub the bread with 1 teaspoon of the olive oil and broil or grill in a panini press to golden. (A broiler or panini press is the best for bruschetta bread because you get a nice golden chewy crust and the center of the bread remains soft. A toaster would dry the bread all the way through.) Rub one side of each piece of bread with the garlic cloves. Discard the garlic. Set 1 piece of bread on each of four plates, garlic side up.

2 | In a large skillet over medium-high heat, add the remaining 2 tablespoons olive oil. Once the oil is hot, drop in the arugula. Using tongs, toss frequently until the arugula starts to wilt—be careful not to overcook. Remove from the heat and sprinkle with a pinch of salt, add the lemon juice, and stir. Spoon the mixture evenly across the 4 pieces of toasted bread.

continued

3 | In another large skillet over medium-high heat, bring about 8 cups of water to a boil with 2 teaspoons salt and the vinegar. (Use a shallow pan so you can see the eggs.) Turn the boiling water to just below a simmer. Crack the eggs into the water. Cook until the white is completely set and the yolk has a thin veil of white set over it and is still soft, about 3 minutes. Use a slotted spoon to pull the eggs out of the water one at a time and blot with a towel to remove the excess water. Place the eggs on top of the arugula.

4 | Drizzle each egg with 1 teaspoon of the truffle oil or olive oil. Sprinkle the Parmesan over each egg. Garnish with the parsley and lemon zest and serve.

CROQUE MADAME

My first croque madame in Paris was an epiphany. Here was a perfectly golden grilled cheese sandwich with bubbly crisp Gruyère cheese, warm ham basking in creamy béchamel sauce, and a perfectly fried egg perched on top, making it a "madame" instead of a "monsieur" (see page 86). Instead of making a flour and butter–thickened cheese sauce (Mornay), this quick version will yield the same wonderfully rich, creamy sensation.

SERVES 4

8	slices white bread		1	teaspoon fresh lemon juice
4	slices boiled ham		1	cup grated Gruyère cheese
⅓	cup heavy cream		2	tablespoons unsalted butter
¼	cup grated Parmesan cheese		4	large eggs
1	teaspoon freshly ground black pepper		2	tablespoons fresh flat-leaf parsley, roughly chopped

1 | Lay 4 pieces of the bread on a sheet pan. Add a slice of ham to each.

2 | Turn on the broiler.

3 | In small saucepan, heat the cream, Parmesan, and pepper until just under a boil. Simmer for 1 minute. Turn off the heat. Stir in the lemon juice and allow to cool for a few minutes. Spoon the sauce evenly across the 4 slices of ham. Place another piece of bread on top of the others.

4 | Distribute the Gruyère evenly over the top of each sandwich. Place under the broiler and watch carefully. Broil until the cheese is golden and melted.

5 | In a large nonstick pan, melt the butter over medium heat. Set each sandwich in the pan and griddle the bottom until golden. Place the sandwiches on plates.

6 | In the same pan, fry the eggs (see Flavor Secrets, page 198). Set 1 egg on top of each sandwich. Garnish with the parsley and serve.

continued

FLAVOR SECRETS

To make the perfect fried egg, melt 1 teaspoon unsalted butter in a nonstick pan over medium heat. Crack the egg(s) into the pan and season with a pinch of salt. Now you have two options: First (my preference), add 1 tablespoon water, cover the pan, and cook to desired doneness, leaving the yolk bright yellow and very soft. Or second, fry until the white goes from clear to opaque, then flip over the egg. (Flipping tip: With a spatula, go under the egg and, with a quick motion, "commit to the flip" like you're flipping a pancake. Don't pause halfway through.) Continue to cook to desired doneness.

CREPE-FRIED PILLOWS WITH GRUYÈRE AND SMOKED PAPRIKA

This is a combination of my family's favorites: eggs and crepes. (This is probably the only recipe that inspires my kids to eat a crepe without Nutella!) When you cut into the golden, tender crepe the yolk oozes out, mixing with the smoked paprika and the melted cheese to create a creamy, fire-roasted sauce. The fillings for these crepe pillows are unlimited—ham, roasted peppers, and your choice of cheese and herbs. And you'll have plenty of extra crepe batter for more eggs and or dessert crepes later.

SERVES 4

6 large eggs

1 large egg yolk

½ cup water

1 cup 2% milk

½ teaspoon kosher salt

1 cup all-purpose flour

4 tablespoons (½ stick) plus 1 teaspoon unsalted butter

4 ounces Manchego cheese, grated

2 tablespoons finely chopped fresh flat-leaf parsley

1 teaspoon smoked paprika

1 | To prepare the crepe batter, in a medium bowl, combine 2 of the eggs, the egg yolk, water, milk, and salt. Whisk just to combine. Whisk in the flour and set aside.

2 | In a medium nonstick skillet over medium heat, melt 4 tablespoons of the butter. Once the butter is melted and golden brown, turn off the heat and let it cool. (When the butter froths and then settles, it's time to turn off the heat. Keep an eye on it as it can go from nutty to burned if you are not careful.) Gently whisk the butter into the batter to combine. The batter is now ready.

3 | In the same nonstick skillet over medium heat, add the remaining 1 teaspoon butter. Once the butter is melted, crack 1 egg into the middle of the pan. Pour ¼ cup of the crepe batter around the egg, allowing the batter to come right up to the egg. Tilt and swirl the pan to get the crepe batter to spread out thinly from the edge of the egg to the edge of the pan. If you don't do this, the batter will pool closer to the egg and you will have a very thick crepe when you form the pillow. When the egg white goes from clear to white, sprinkle some of the Manchego over the egg. Use a spatula to fold the crepe over the yolk from each of four sides to form a pillow over the yolk. Flip over the pillow. Cook for 1 more minute. Remove the pillow from the pan and set on a plate.

4 | Repeat this process for the remaining 3 eggs. Garnish with some parsley and smoked paprika. Serve immediately.

CHILAQUILES

I first had this breakfast on a beach in Mexico: corn tortilla chips simmered in salsa, with a slight crunch on the edges and a chew in the center. You get intense freshness from the salsa's acidity and mild heat, and creamy goodness from the egg yolk. A finishing garnish of queso fresco (feta cheese can be substituted) is always great in this dish that's super for breakfast, lunch, or dinner. If it's the right time, throw in a Michalada (Mexican beer on ice with lime, a splash of Tabasco, and a salted rim)!

SERVES 2 TO 4

1	pound tomatillos
1	tablespoon canola oil
1	cup finely chopped white onions
2	teaspoons finely chopped garlic
½	teaspoon ground cumin
½	teaspoon dried Mexican oregano
⅔	cup fresh cilantro, roughly chopped
1	serrano chile
2	teaspoons kosher salt, plus more for seasoning
4	cups thick, firm corn tortilla chips
1	tablespoon unsalted butter
4	large eggs
¼	cup crumbled queso fresco or feta cheese

1 | Take the husks off the tomatillos and discard. Rinse the tomatillos under warm water and rub off the sticky film. Place in a medium pot and cover with cold water. Bring to a boil and simmer until dark green but *not* split, about 6 minutes. Drain carefully so you don't break the tomatillos and lose their precious juice. Transfer to a blender.

2 | In a medium skillet over medium heat, add the canola oil. Once the oil is hot, add the onions and garlic and cook until slightly golden. Add the cumin and oregano and stir just to toast the spices. Transfer to the blender.

3 | Add ⅓ cup of the cilantro, the serrano, and salt to the blender. (Use half the serrano for less heat.) Puree the mixture to a smooth sauce. Set aside.

4 | In a large skillet over medium heat, toss the tortilla chips with the sauce just until the chips start to soften. Transfer to a serving dish.

continued

5 | In a medium nonstick skillet over medium heat, melt the butter. Crack in the eggs and sprinkle with a touch of salt. When the whites set, flip over the eggs and cook for 30 seconds more. Flip the eggs again and place on top of the tortillas and sauce. (If you prefer not to flip the eggs, add a tablespoon of water to the side of the pan and cover to cook.)

6 | Garnish with the remaining ⅓ cup chopped cilantro and the queso fresco. Serve immediately.

FLAVOR SECRETS

For an oven version of the same recipe, place the chips in a baking dish. Crack the eggs on top of the chips (carefully, so the yolks don't break). Bring the sauce to a boil and pour it over the eggs and chips. Place the dish in a 300°F oven and bake until the eggs are cooked to the desired doneness.

EGGS PARMIGIANA

Classic Parmigiana flavor is taken to a whole new level in this recipe. The egg yolk creates a rich center that unites with the slightly sweet, sharp tomato sauce, the crunch of bread, the bright, mild anise perfume of the basil, and the decadent finishing flavor of nutty Parmesan and creamy mozzarella.

SERVES 4

1	tablespoon olive oil or unsalted butter
4	large eggs
	Kosher salt
1½	cups tomato sauce

12	fresh basil leaves
1	cup shredded fresh mozzarella cheese
⅓	cup grated Parmesan cheese

1 | Preheat the oven to broil.

2 | In a large nonstick ovenproof skillet over medium heat, add the olive oil. Crack the eggs carefully into the pan. Season with a touch of salt. Turn down the heat a little bit so that the eggs are not bubbling. Cook until firm but with a very soft yolk. Add the tomato sauce evenly over the eggs. Sprinkle evenly with the basil. Sprinkle with the mozzarella and Parmesan.

3 | Place the skillet, uncovered, in the oven. Broil until the cheese is melted and golden. The egg yolk should still be soft (cook longer if you like it firmer).

4 | Using a spatula, place an egg on each of four plates and serve.

FLAVOR SECRETS

For great flavor contrasts, add black olives for briny saltiness and chile flakes for heat. Add bread crumbs on top with the cheese for a crispy topping.

HARISSA-BAKED EGGS WITH FETA, MINT, AND BLACK OLIVES

Harissa's fiery flavor blends with eggs to yield a luscious sauce. The feta adds creaminess and a rich, cleansing saltiness complemented by the mint and olives.

SERVES 2 TO 4

2½	tablespoons olive oil	2	tablespoons harissa
4	large eggs	2	cups canned chopped tomatoes with their juices
	Kosher salt and freshly ground black pepper	2	cups chicken stock
1	teaspoon chopped garlic	½	cup crumbled feta cheese
½	cup black olives, pitted and roughly chopped	1	cup Bush's Best garbanzo beans, rinsed and drained
¼	cup fresh mint leaves, roughly sliced	½	teaspoon cumin seed

1 | Preheat the oven to 300°F.

2 | Rub four ramekins with 1½ teaspoons of the olive oil. Crack 1 egg into each dish. Sprinkle lightly with salt and pepper.

3 | In a medium skillet over medium heat, add another 1½ teaspoons of the olive oil. Once the oil is hot, add the garlic, black olives, and mint (save a little of the mint for garnish). Stir just until you smell the garlic but do not brown it. Add the harissa, tomatoes, and chicken stock. Cook for 2 minutes at just below a simmer.

4 | Spoon the mixture evenly over the eggs. It is *very* important that you pour the sauce over the eggs right away while it is still hot, so that the egg whites cook before the yolks get hard. Scatter the feta evenly over the top. Place the ramekins on a baking sheet and tent with foil (this will prevent the yolks from overcooking) and bake for about 10 minutes, or until the eggs are cooked to your desired doneness. Remember, the eggs will continue to cook slightly due to the residual heat after they are removed from the oven.

5 | While the eggs are baking, make sure the garbanzo beans are dry. Roughly chop.

6 | In a separate medium nonstick pan over medium-high heat, add the remaining 1½ tablespoons olive oil. Once the oil is hot, add the garbanzo beans. Fry until golden and crispy, about 4 minutes. Turn off the heat. Stir in the cumin seed and a pinch of salt. Transfer to a plate to cool.

7 | Remove the ramekins from the oven and place each one on a plate lined with a damp napkin to prevent it from slipping. Divide the garbanzos over the top and garnish with a touch of the reserved sliced mint.

SCRAMBLED EGGS WITH SAUTÉED PANCETTA, RADICCHIO, AND LEMON

This recipe evokes the tastes of Italy. Light, fluffy scrambled eggs laced with strands of slightly bitter sautéed radicchio come together with lemon and peppery pancetta.

SERVES 4

6   large eggs
¼   cup plus 2 tablespoons water
¼   teaspoon kosher salt
1   teaspoon olive oil
¼   cup finely cubed pancetta
    (or substitute bacon, ham,
    or prosciutto)

2   cups roughly sliced radicchio
2   tablespoons fresh lemon juice
1   teaspoon unsalted butter

1 | In a small bowl, whisk the eggs, water, and salt together. Set aside.

2 | In a medium skillet over medium heat, add the olive oil. Add the pancetta and cook until golden but not overly crispy, about 3 minutes. Add the radicchio and sauté until the radicchio softens and becomes slightly golden, about 3 minutes. Pour in the lemon juice, stir, and turn off the heat.

3 | In a large nonstick skillet over medium heat, melt the butter. Add the whisked eggs and allow to set for about 15 seconds. Using a rubber spatula, "paint" the bottom of the pan, lifting the egg and creating folds. Allow the liquid to run into the painted spaces. Once the egg is mostly set but is still wet, turn off the heat and fold in the pancetta-radicchio mixture. Place on plates right away to avoid overcooking the egg in the residual heat of the pan. Serve immediately.

FLAVOR SECRETS

Great scrambled eggs love moderate to low heat. Use a spatula to lift and fold the eggs instead of stirring. Adding water to the eggs (1 tablespoon of water and a pinch of salt per egg) creates steam and adds fluffiness.

BREAD CRUMB—FRIED EGGS WITH CRISPY SALAMI BITS (SCOTCH EGGS OVER EASY)

A Scotch egg is a partially hard-cooked egg that's rolled in ground meat and bread crumbs and then deep-fried. It's about as rich and decadent as an egg can get, and this version takes only minutes to make.

SERVES 2

¼ cup sliced salami

¼ cup bread crumbs

½ teaspoon anise seed

2 teaspoons unsalted butter

2 large eggs

1 tablespoon finely chopped fresh flat-leaf parsley

1 | In a food processor, combine the salami, bread crumbs, and anise seed and pulse-chop to a crumble.

2 | In a small nonstick skillet over medium heat, melt 1 teaspoon of the butter. Crack in the eggs. Cook over easy or as you like them and remove from the heat. Place on a serving plate and set aside.

3 | Add the remaining 1 teaspoon butter to the skillet. When the butter is melted, add the salami mixture and stir for 1 minute, until golden brown. Spoon over the eggs. Garnish with the parsley and serve.

BACON AND GRUYÈRE QUICHE

Gruyère, bacon, and eggs are true soul mates. In this version—a balance between a hotel brunch and a trip to Paris—the quiche is cooked until the eggs are just set, not a moment longer. The crust is buttery and perfectly golden. The fontina adds a fondue quality to the texture, and the Gruyère adds a sharp nuttiness. If you desire, leeks softened in butter or olive oil add a moistness and subtle onion flavor.

SERVES 6

- 1 frozen piecrust
- 2 large leeks (optional)
- 2 teaspoons butter (for the leeks, if using)
- 6 large eggs
- 1¼ cups half-and-half (or heavy cream for full French richness)
- ½ teaspoon kosher salt
- ⅓ teaspoon ground white pepper
- Pinch of ground nutmeg (ideally, freshly grated)
- 6 slices thick-cut applewood-smoked bacon, cooked, cut into ½-inch pieces
- 1 ounce fontina cheese, shredded (about ¼ cup)
- 3 ounces Gruyère cheese, shredded (about ¾ cup)

1 | Bake your piecrust according to the package instructions. For a perfect crust, cover the edges of the crust with aluminum foil about halfway through baking so that the bottom can get golden without overcooking the edges. Set aside to cool.

2 | Preheat the oven to 350°F.

3 | If using the leeks, cut the dark green parts of the leeks off and discard. Cut the leeks lengthwise in half and pull out the yellow hard core. Discard. Rinse the leeks under cold water, then slice the leeks crosswise into thin little half-moon shapes. In a medium nonstick skillet, melt the butter. Add the leeks. Cook, stirring occasionally, until soft, about 8 minutes. Manage the heat so that the leeks do not get golden or crispy. (You may have to turn down the heat to low after the first couple of minutes.) Set aside to cool.

4 | In a medium bowl, whisk together the eggs, half-and-half, salt, white pepper, and nutmeg. Set aside for a few minutes. This sitting time will allow the air bubbles to escape, resulting in a custardlike, moist filling.

5 | Sprinkle the bottom of the cooled piecrust evenly with the bacon, fontina, Gruyère, and leeks, if using. Slowly pour the custard over the top in an even pattern to keep all the ingredients evenly dispersed. Set the quiche on a sheet pan and place in the oven. Bake, uncovered, for 30 minutes, or until there is a circle the size of a quarter in the center that is still jiggly. The residual carryover heat will finish cooking the quiche as it cools. Remove from the oven and transfer to a cooling rack or stone countertop to cool for 15 minutes.

6 | Once the quiche has cooled, cut it into pie-style slices and serve by itself or with a mixed green salad. Quiche is great hot, at room temperature, or cold.

FLAVOR SECRETS

Experiment with your own choice of meats, cheeses, and veggies. The key is to stick to a ratio of 1¼ cups dairy to 6 eggs so the custard comes out right. Bear in mind that fattier cheeses will make the custard smoother and add richness. Drier, aged cheeses will add more flavor but create a less rich filling.

SWEET AND SPICY HOISIN-GLAZED STEAK AND EGGS

This flavor-packed dish will sate any appetite. There's the sweetness of hoisin sauce, the heat of Sriracha, the glaze of juicy seared meat, the little bursts of sesame nuttiness, and an egg yolk that creates a sauce that years of chef's training can't replicate. Are you hungry yet?

SERVES 4

1	tablespoon sesame seeds	3	tablespoons low-sodium soy sauce
2	teaspoons peanut oil	2	teaspoons Sriracha sauce
One	10-ounce skirt steak	2	teaspoons unsalted butter
	Kosher salt and freshly ground black pepper	4	large eggs
		¼	cup roughly chopped fresh cilantro
¼	cup hoisin sauce	¼	cup roughly chopped green onions

1 | In a small dry skillet over medium-high heat, toast the sesame seeds and transfer to a plate to cool.

2 | In a medium nonstick skillet over medium-high heat, add the peanut oil. Pat the steak dry and season with salt and pepper. Sear the bottom of the steak in the skillet until dark golden, about 3 minutes.

3 | Meanwhile, in a small bowl, mix together the hoisin, soy, and Sriracha sauces to create a glaze.

4 | Flip over the steak. Rub the hoisin glaze on top of the steak. Flip over again and cook for 30 seconds more or to the desired doneness. Remove the steak from the skillet and set aside on a plate to rest.

5 | In a medium nonstick skillet over medium heat, add the butter. Once the butter is melted, crack in the eggs and sprinkle with a pinch of salt. When the whites start to set, flip over the eggs. Cook to desired doneness. Flip again and set on the plate next to the steak. Garnish with the cilantro, green onions, and sesame seeds and serve.

FLAVOR SECRETS

You can use any type of steak you like. I like the full flavor and low price of skirt. New York strip makes a more elegant dish; rib-eye steak makes a richer dish because of its higher fat content. Filet mignon is very tender but not as flavorful as the skirt steak.

SWEET TOOTH

...

CARAMELIZED BUTTER AND SEA SALT CHOCOLATE CHIP COOKIES 216

FIVE-SPICE FRENCH TOAST WITH ICE CREAM 218

ALMOND-ORANGE-CHOCOLATE BISCOTTI 221

ESPRESSO GRANITA WITH MASCARPONE CREAM 223

TIRAMISÙ 224

CARDAMOM-SPICED FLAMED RED BANANAS 227

NUTELLA CREPES 229

My sweetest food memories are simple indulgences at my paternal grandparents' big summerhouse on a lake in Wisconsin—a place called the House of Seven Gables. (It doesn't get more idyllic than that.) My grandmother, who was way ahead of Ben & Jerry's, used to stir chunks of Milky Way candy bars into homemade vanilla ice cream that she hand-churned in a tub with rock salt. She'd make incredible fluffy pancakes and give my sisters and me pocket money to buy candy at a local store. We spent half the summer happily popping back Milk Duds, Whoppers, and licorice.

Thankfully my sweet tooth has grown up over the years. I've traded in Milk Duds and licorice sticks for Nutella Crepes (page 229) and Cardamom-Spiced Flamed Red Bananas (page 227). I satisfy my malted milk chocolate cravings with Caramelized Butter and Sea Salt Chocolate Chip Cookies (page 216). And my Five-Spice French Toast with Ice Cream (page 218) pays homage to my beloved Chinese food.

The recipes in this chapter have enough whimsy and sweetness to satisfy adults and kids alike. Good luck trying to limit yourself to just one (or two!) a day.

CARAMELIZED BUTTER AND SEA SALT CHOCOLATE CHIP COOKIES

My daughter and I had a ton of fun (and consumed far too much cookie dough) coming up with this ultimate chocolate chip cookie recipe. These cookies are the best of sweet, salty, and decadent. Minimally mixing the batter makes for a flat, chewy cookie with a distinct toasted nut and cooked sugar flavor heightened by nuggets of rich chocolate and the slightly salty/minerally finish of the sea salt. I prefer to chop Scharffenberger's 60% dark chocolate into these treats, but feel free to swap in the chocolate of your choice.

MAKES THIRTEEN 5-INCH COOKIES

½   pound (2 sticks) unsalted butter

½   cup granulated sugar

½   cup light brown sugar (not packed)

½   cup dark brown sugar (not packed)

½   vanilla bean, split lengthwise, or 1 teaspoon pure vanilla extract

2   large eggs

2   cups all-purpose flour

1   teaspoon baking soda

1   teaspoon kosher salt

6   ounces (1 cup) semisweet chocolate chips or chopped chunks

2   tablespoons sea salt

1 | Preheat the oven to 350°F. Line two light-colored baking sheets with parchment paper and set aside. (Dark cookie sheets will cause the cookies to get too dark on the bottom.)

2 | In a medium nonstick skillet over medium heat, melt one stick of butter until it turns brown and begins to smell nutty. As it melts, the butter will foam up. This is your sign that the milk solids are starting to brown. As soon as the foam starts to fade, turn off the heat (the butter should be a light brown color). The residual heat of the pan will darken the butter further without burning it. Using a rubber spatula, transfer the brown butter to the bowl of an electric stand mixer. Set aside until cool to the touch. Cut the remaining one stick of butter into 1-inch cubes and set aside to come to room temperature.

3 | Add the room-temperature butter to the mixing bowl with the cooled brown butter. Into the same bowl, add the granulated sugar, light brown sugar, and dark brown sugar. Using the paddle attachment of the mixer, beat the mixture slowly until the butter and sugar start to come together, about 30 seconds. Turn the mixer speed to medium-high and continue beating until evenly mixed, about 2 minutes. Be careful not to overmix the batter and incorporate air bubbles.

4 | Use the back of a knife to scrape the seeds of the vanilla bean into a separate small bowl (or pour the vanilla extract into the bowl). Crack the eggs into this bowl and stir just to mix. Pour the eggs into the butter mixture and mix on low just to combine.

5 | In a separate medium bowl, whisk together the flour, baking soda, and salt. With the mixer on low speed, add the flour mixture to the mixing bowl in a constant, steady stream—quickly. Mix just until combined. Add the chocolate chips and mix on low just until combined.

6 | Using a 4-ounce ice cream scoop or a ½-cup measure, drop mounds of dough onto the sheet pans, spacing the dough 3 inches apart (roughly 6 cookies per sheet). Press down on the dough to flatten each cookie to about ⅓ inch thick. Sprinkle the tops evenly with a pinch of the sea salt. Place in the oven and bake for about 10 minutes, or until golden brown and still soft in the center. Rotate the pans halfway through baking.

7 | Remove from the oven and allow to cool for 1 minute. Use a spatula to place the cookies on a cool platter.

FLAVOR SECRETS

The cookies continue to harden and darken as they cool, so I always recommend taking them out of the oven when they are a little softer than you think they should be. Your cookies will come out perfectly every time!

FIVE-SPICE FRENCH TOAST WITH ICE CREAM

What could be better than breakfast for dessert? Five-spice powder creates an "adult" cinnamon toast with a spicy (but not hot) crust on the outside of thick, golden bread. The star anise and pepper in the five-spice powder play nicely with the chocolate sauce. The outside is chewy and sweet. The inside is like a crème brûlée, with a creamy egg custard center. And the ice cream? Taste and see for yourself.

SERVES 2 TO 4

3 large eggs
½ cup half-and-half
2 tablespoons sugar
1 teaspoon pure vanilla extract
1 teaspoon five-spice powder
1 teaspoon kosher salt

2 tablespoons unsalted butter plus more as needed
4 slices rustic bread (with crust)
4 scoops vanilla ice cream
½ cup chocolate syrup

1 | In a large bowl, mix together the eggs, half-and-half, sugar, vanilla, five-spice powder, and salt.

2 | In a griddle or large nonstick pan over medium heat, melt the butter.

3 | Submerge the bread in the egg mixture and hold for 3 seconds to allow the egg to soak in. Pull each slice out and allow the excess egg to drip off. Place the coated bread on the hot griddle. Cook until deep golden brown on each side, about 3 minutes per side. Repeat with the other slices, adding more butter to the griddle as necessary.

4 | Set one slice on each of four plates. Top with a scoop of ice cream and drizzle with the chocolate syrup. Serve immediately.

ALMOND-ORANGE-CHOCOLATE BISCOTTI

Biscotti, the word derived from the Latin for "twice-baked," owe their dry, crunchy texture to that very double cooking process. Enjoy one of these irresistible cookies on its own or let it melt in your mouth after dipping it into a cup of coffee or a cappuccino. I love the rich almond flavor accented by the bright flavor of orange zest. Perfect for breakfast *and* dessert.

MAKES ABOUT 24 BISCOTTI

2¾ cups all-purpose flour, plus more for dusting	3 large eggs
1⅔ cups sugar	4 large egg yolks
1 teaspoon kosher salt	1 teaspoon pure vanilla extract
1 teaspoon baking powder	3 ounces bittersweet chocolate, shaved
1 teaspoon anise seed	6 ounces skin-on sliced or slivered almonds
1 orange	

1 | Preheat the oven to 350°F. Line two baking sheets with parchment paper and set aside.

2 | In the bowl of an electric stand mixer, stir together the flour, sugar, salt, baking powder, and anise seed. Zest the orange into the mixture and stir to combine.

3 | In a separate bowl, whisk together the eggs, egg yolks, and vanilla.

4 | Fit the stand mixer with the paddle attachment. Pour the egg mixture into the flour mixture and mix on low just to combine. Turn off the mixer and add the chocolate and almonds. Turn on the mixer to low and mix just to combine. The dough should be sticky enough that it sticks to your hands but not so sticky that you can't get it off in a large lump.

5 | Dust a countertop with flour. Use a spatula to remove the dough from the mixer and place it on the floured counter. Separate the dough into three even piles. Roll each pile into the shape of a log. Do not overwork the dough. The key to these yummy cookies is to make sure the dough is moist enough that it wants to stick to the counter and your hands but not so moist that you cannot work with it. Add more flour if needed.

continued

6 | Place the logs evenly spaced on one of the parchment-lined baking sheets. (The dough will expand when baking.) Bake until the logs form the shape of a half-moon and become golden with soft centers, about 20 minutes. Remove from the oven and slide the logs onto a cooling rack to cool.

7 | Turn down the heat to 300°F.

8 | Once the logs are cool, use a bread knife to slice each log crosswise as if cutting a loaf of bread, yielding half-moon (biscotti-shaped) cookies. Lay the cookies on the parchment-lined baking sheets and place in the oven. After 10 minutes, rotate the baking sheets halfway. Bake for 10 more minutes, or until the centers of the cookies give ever so slightly to your fingernail. If too soft, they will be chewy. If too hard, they will be overly crunchy and dry.

9 | Remove from the oven and let cool. Store in an airtight container at room temperature.

ESPRESSO GRANITA WITH MASCARPONE CREAM

This dish has surprised many guests in the best way. The espresso is clean and full flavored. The mascarpone turns it into a mouthful of iced latte.

5   cups water
1   cup espresso beans, finely ground
¼   cup vanilla syrup
½   cup heavy cream

3   tablespoons sugar
½   cup mascarpone cheese
    Pinch of kosher salt
¼   cup shaved semisweet chocolate

1 | In a medium saucepan set over high heat, bring the water to a boil. Stir in the ground espresso. Remove from the heat, cover, and let sit for 10 minutes. Strain through a coffee filter into a bowl. (You can also make 5 cups of strong coffee any other way you like.) Add the vanilla syrup and stir.

2 | Pour the coffee into a 9 x 12-inch or similar size baking dish. Allow to cool to room temperature. Cover the dish with aluminum foil and place in the freezer. Every 20 minutes, run a fork through the mixture to create shards of ice.

3 | Keep an eye on the granita for the first 30 minutes. It's important to run the fork through it before it sets into one hard block. Once you have run the fork through a few times and have nice shards, you can leave it alone. Keep it covered tightly.

4 | In the bowl of an electric stand mixer fitted with the whisk attachment, beat the cream at medium speed until soft peaks form. Slowly add 1 tablespoon of the sugar, mixing until soft peaks form. Take the whipped cream out of the bowl and set aside.

5 | In the same bowl with the same whisk, whip the mascarpone, salt, and the remaining 2 tablespoons sugar for 1 minute. Add the whipped cream to the mascarpone and whip gently just until combined. Cover tightly and refrigerate until ready to serve.

6 | To serve, set the mascarpone cream out on the counter about 15 minutes before serving. Take a metal spoon and break up the granita. Spoon the granita into martini-style glasses and place a scoop of the cream on top of each serving. Sprinkle the chocolate over the top. Serve immediately.

TIRAMISÙ

Many years ago while I was in culinary school, I wrote a letter to a famous chef in England and offered, "I'll come to London and work seven days and nights for free—what do you think?" He accepted. My fondest memory during that intense period was working with the pastry chef at 5:00 A.M. making a version of this tiramisù. The ladyfingers melt into the mascarpone cream, leaving behind just a bit of texture. The espresso is bold and cuts through the rich egg-and-sugar cream.

SERVES 12

5	large eggs	1	cup coffee beans (or pre-ground coffee)
¼	cup plus ⅓ cup sugar	4	cups water
16	ounces mascarpone cheese, at room temperature	32	ladyfingers
		½	cup bittersweet cocoa powder

1 | Separate the egg yolks and egg whites into two bowls. In the bowl of an electric stand mixer fitted with the whisk attachment, add the egg whites and mix until the whites are foamy. Then slowly add ¼ cup of the sugar while the mixer is running. The key is to *stop* when the egg whites are at medium peak. (If you overwhip, your egg whites will break down and the mascarpone cream will get watery.) Using a rubber spatula, transfer the whipped whites to a separate medium bowl.

2 | Clean the mixer bowl and add the remaining ⅓ cup sugar and the egg yolks and beat with the whisk attachment on medium until pale yellow and fluffy. With the mixer still on medium speed, add one spoonful of the mascarpone at a time until fully incorporated and smooth.

3 | Stir a large scoop of the egg whites into the mascarpone mixture. Fold the remaining whites into the mixture until smooth and evenly distributed. Chill the mixture in the refrigerator for up to an hour, until needed.

4 | Grind the coffee beans or use coffee that is pre-ground for a coffee machine, not for espresso. Good coffee with a dark roast is best. In a medium saucepan, bring the water to a boil and turn off the heat. Add the coffee and stir. Cover and let sit for 15 minutes. Strain the coffee through a fine-mesh strainer and discard the solids. Return the coffee to the pot and boil until you have 3 cups of liquid.

5 | In a medium casserole dish, spread half the mascarpone cream.

continued

6 | Dip the ladyfingers, 2 at a time, into the hot coffee (cool it enough that you don't burn yourself). Soak for only 2 seconds, until the cookies fully absorb the coffee but do not fall apart. When you pull them out of the hot coffee, turn them over and watch the coffee get absorbed; the cookies should be thoroughly soaked but not be so firm that they're easy to handle.

7 | Lay the soaked cookies in the cream, resting on their sides. You should be able to fit about two rows' worth and then possibly one sideways row to complete the dish.

8 | Pour the remainder of the cream over the cookies and smooth it out evenly. Cover the casserole tightly with plastic wrap, being careful to keep the plastic off the surface of the cream. Place in the refrigerator to set for at least 2 hours.

9 | Use a spatula or large spoon to scoop a portion onto each plate. Sprinkle with the cocoa powder, using a strainer to allow even dusting.

CARDAMOM-SPICED FLAMED RED BANANAS

I made my first bananas Foster *à la française* in a little apartment in Paris. This variation is super delicious and super simple. Red bananas taste like tropical fruit and are a little more dense and creamy than their yellow counterparts. My kids love this dessert because of the show (the flames rise more than a foot high!). Though I've never had a problem with it, I still recommend using caution and keeping the kids back a few feet. If you're wary, skip the flame and stick with the rest of the dessert. (You can leave out the alcohol if you prefer.)

SERVES 4

2 red bananas (regular bananas OK)

¼ teaspoon cardamom seed, ground

3 tablespoons butter

2 tablespoons brown sugar

Pinch of kosher salt

¼ cup orange liqueur (optional)

¼ cup fresh orange juice (1 orange)

4 large scoops vanilla ice cream

1 | Peel the bananas and cut on a slight angle into ½-inch-thick slices.

2 | In a large nonstick skillet over medium-high heat, add the cardamom and butter. When the butter is melted, add the brown sugar and salt, and stir. Add the bananas and stir. Let them sit and caramelize for about 2 minutes.

3 | (If you don't want the flames, skip the next step and just pour the liqueur directly into the center of the pan and stir gently. Or leave out the orange liqueur, if desired.)

4 | Tilt the pan back so the mixture slides toward you and the opposite end of the pan is directly over the heat. Tilt the pan flat again and add the orange liqueur to the empty side of the pan. Tilt it slightly toward the flame to ignite the alcohol. You will get a big flame that burns off quickly as the alcohol evaporates.

5 | Pour the orange juice onto the flame to put it out, or enjoy the show for about 20 seconds until it goes out by itself and then pour on the orange juice. Stir.

6 | Spoon the ice cream into four bowls and top with the bananas. Serve immediately.

NUTELLA CREPES

Crepe stands are as prevalent in Paris as doughnut shops are in America. Batter is poured onto a griddle and spread thin with a wooden tool called a *râteau*. The crepe bubbles and then settles and turns golden brown. The Nutella (hazelnut and chocolate whipped into a luscious creamy spread) is slathered on the crepe. Once hard to find in America, Nutella is now available in most supermarkets. One of life's simple pleasures!

SERVES 5

6	tablespoons unsalted butter	1	cup milk
2	large eggs	½	teaspoon kosher salt
1	large egg yolk	1	cup all-purpose flour
½	cup water	½	cup Nutella

1 | In a medium nonstick pan over medium heat, melt the butter. Once the butter is melted, continue cooking until the butter is golden brown. Remove from the heat and set aside. The residual heat will make the butter a little more brown, so err on the side of golden brown versus dark before you turn off the heat.

2 | In a medium bowl, gently whisk together the eggs, egg yolk, water, milk, and salt until just combined. Add the flour and whisk until smooth. Slowly pour the browned butter into the mixture, whisking constantly. If necessary, strain the mixture to remove any lumps.

3 | Use a paper towel to wipe out the same nonstick pan used to melt the butter. Set the pan over medium heat. Using a ⅓-cup measure, scoop the batter and pour it into the center of the hot pan. Using a rotating motion with your wrist, swirl the batter around and out to the edges of the pan—the thinner, the better. Return the pan to the heat and cook for 2 minutes. Use a rubber spatula to lift up the edge of the crepe and flip the crepe over. Cook on the other side for 30 seconds to 1 minute, depending on how golden you like it.

4 | Slide the crepe onto a plate and spread with 1 tablespoon of the Nutella (or as much as you like). Fold the crepe in half, then fold in half again to form a triangle. You can also just roll up the crepe loosely like a carpet. Garnish with desired toppings.

INDEX

...

White Pepper Cassoulet, 92–93
French Toast, Five-Spice, with Ice Cream, 218–219
Fusilli with Fennel Seed–Oregano Chicken, Mushrooms, and Cream Sauce, 64–65

G
Garam masala, xiv, 5, 146, 147, 149, 151
Garam Masala Chicken Pot Pie, 163–165
Garlic, 31, 101, 102–103, 139–140
Garlic and Black Pepper Surf and Turf Stir-Fry, 139–140
Ginger, 123, 146
Ginger-Spiced Chicken Tikka Sandwich with Cumin-Tomato Mayo, 151–153
Goat cheese (*see* Cheese)
Gochujang, 126, 127
Gorgonzola and Caramelized Pear and Goat Cheese Sandwich, 57–59
Green Chile Chutney, 22–24
Grilled Achiote Veggie Tostadas with Goat Cheese, 10–12
Grilled Chicken with Tarragon-Roasted Tomatoes, 184–185, 187
Grilled Corn with Cilantro Pesto and Cotija Cheese, 8–9
Grilled Radicchio with Balsamic Vinegar, Parmesan, and Sea Salt, 172
Grilled Tilapia in Spicy Asian Broth, 138
Grove's Bourbon, Bacon, Allspice Chili, 178–179

H
Halloumi cheese, 154
Harissa, 29
Harissa:
    Harissa and Green Onion Chicken Salad Sandwiches, 39
    Harissa-Baked Eggs with Feta, Mint, and Black Olives, 204–205
    Harissa mayo, 188–189
    Harissa-Roasted Baba Ghanoush, 30
    Harissa Steak Sandwiches, 40–41
Herbes de Provence, xv, 75, 76, 77, 86, 88, 92–93
Herbs, xiv–xv, 51. (*see also specific herbs*)
Hoisin, 123, 124–125, 134, 210–211
Hot-and-Sour Soup, 130
Hummus:
    Roasted-Garlic and Toasted-Cumin Hummus with Smoked-Paprika Pita, 31

I
Ice Cream, Five-Spice French Toast with, 218–219

Indian recipes:
    Crispy Cheese and Sweet Peas in Indian-Spiced Tomato Sauce, 154–155
    Curried Sweet Pea Soup with Buttered White Pepper Bread Crumbs, 150
    Dal with Garam Masala, 149
    Garam Masala Chicken Pot Pie, 163–165
    Ginger-Spiced Chicken Tikka Sandwich with Cumin-Tomato Mayo, 151–153
    Sweet and Spicy Red Chile and Cucumber Raita, 148
    Tandoori-Style Chicken with Basmati Rice and Spicy Tomato Chutney, 161–162
    Three-Spice Shrimp on Curried Yellow Split Peas, 159–160
    Turmeric Grilled Scallop Pitas, 156–158
    Whole Tandoori Chicken with Mustard Seed-Roasted Potatoes, 166–167
Individual Smoked Paprika Lasagnas, 118–119
Italian parsley, 101
Italian recipes:
    Butternut Squash and Roasted Brussels Sprouts Risotto, 53–55
    Classic Tomato-Basil Bruschetta, 52
    Farfalle with Black Olives, Shaved Pecorino, and Lemon, 60–61
    Fusilli with Fennel Seed-Oregano Chicken, Mushrooms, and Cream Sauce, 64–65
    Gorgonzola and Caramelized Pear and Goat Cheese Sandwich, 57–59
    Open-Face Lasagna with Morel Mushrooms and Asparagus, 62–63
    Osso Bucco, 70–71
    Penne Bolognese, 68–69
    Pork Chops with Caramelized Apples and Arugula, 66–67
    White Bean Soup with Rosemary Pesto, 56

J
Jalapeño, xv, 5, 23–24, 136, 148, 174–175
Jeffrey's Spicy Margarita, 12

K
Kale:
    Sautéed Kale with Walnut Oil, Lemon Juice, and Chili Flakes, 183
Kasseri cheese, 154

Kibbee, Sumac-Spiced, 46–47
Kosher salt, xi

L
Lamb (*see* Meat)
Lasagna:
    Individual Smoked Paprika Lasagnas, 118–119
Leeks:
    Asian Turkey Burgers, 134–135
Lemon:
    Farfalle with Black Olives, Shaved Pecorino, and Lemon, 60–61
    Scrambled Eggs with Sautéed Pancetta, Radicchio, and Lemon, 206
    Sumac-Grilled Salmon with Thyme, Toasted Sesame Seeds, and Lemon, 43
Lemon-Sumac Dressing, 34–35
Lentils:
    Persian Beef/Eggplant Stew (*Gheimeh Bademjan*), 36–37
Lime zest, x
Lobster Pot Pie with Fava Beans, Tarragon, and Coriander Butter Crust, 180–181

M
Margaritas:
    Jeffrey's Spicy Margarita, 12
Meat:. (*see also* Pork)
    Beef Kebabs with Sumac and Roasted Tomato Rice, 44–45
    Garlic and Black Pepper Surf and Turf Stir-Fry, 139–140
    Penne Bolognese, 68–69
    Persian Beef/Eggplant Stew (*Gheimeh Bademjan*), 36–37
    Spicy Beef Pad Thai, 141–142
    Steak Salad with Almond-Basil Dressing, 176
    Strip Steak with "Secret" Green Sauce, 94
    Sumac-Spiced Kibbee, 46–47
    Sweet and Spicy Hoisin-Glazed Steak and Eggs, 210–211
    White Pepper Cassoulet, 92–93
Mexican oregano, x, 5
Mexican recipes:
    Achiote Chicken Sandwich, 25
    Achiote Chicken Stew with Spicy Pickled Red Onions, 13–14
    Anise Seed–Crusted Tilapia Tacos with Five-Minute Mole Sauce, 20–21
    Crab Tostadas with Fire-Roasted Chiles, Avocado, and Tomatillo Salsa, 18–19

ABOUT THE AUTHORS

JEFFREY SAAD is the star of *United Tastes of America,* which debuted on the Cooking Channel in November 2010. He is the executive chef and partner at The Grove, San Francisco's living room, offering gourmet comfort food with a twist. Enamored with food and formally trained at the Culinary Institute of America and the California Culinary Academy, Saad opened the Sweet Heat Mexican restaurant chain in San Francisco and became a partner in Pasta Pomodoro Italian Restaurants, helping to open and operate the first twelve locations in California. In 2009 he was the runner-up on season five of *The Next Food Network Star.* Saad's love and curiosity about different cuisines and cultures have led him on many travels: from China (where he fell in love with the art of cooking in the wok) and dozens of trips to Mexico (where he finds a new chile every time), to France (where he gets inspired to put a spin on the classics), and all throughout Spain (where he discovered his dream come true: small plates of amazing food all day long!). Although he hasn't been to his wife's native Iran or his own native Lebanon, he embraces the flavors of these countries as if he had lived there. A super-engaged family man, second-degree black belt in Tae Kwon Do, surfer, and endless student, Saad lives in Los Angeles with his wife and two children.

DEBRA OLLIVIER is the author of numerous essays and two books, including the national bestseller *What French Women Know: About Love, Sex, and Other Matters of the Heart and Mind.* Through her travels and many years spent living in France, she has learned the true communal pleasures and simple but exalted joys of food.